AUTHENTIC
POLISH
COOKING

AUTHENTIC POLISH COOKING

150 MOUTHWATERING RECIPES, FROM OLD-COUNTRY STAPLES TO EXQUISITE MODERN CUISINE

EDITED BY MARIANNA DWORAK

Skyhorse Publishing

Skyhorse Publishing books may be purchased in bulk at special discounts for sales promotion, corporate gifts, fund-raising, or educational purposes. Special editions can also be created to specifications. For details, contact the Special Sales Department, Skyhorse Publishing, 307 West 36th Street, 11th Floor, New York, NY 10018 or info@skyhorsepublishing.com.

Skyhorse® and Skyhorse Publishing® are registered trademarks of Skyhorse Publishing, Inc.®, a Delaware corporation.

www.skyhorsepublishing.com

10 9 8 7 6 5 4 3 2

Library of Congress Cataloging-in-Publication data is on file.

ISBN: 978-1-62087-091-4

Printed in China

INTRODUCTION

Polish cuisine is hearty and filling, and though some may think the Polish diet is all meat and potatoes, that is far from the truth. Many dishes found on the traditional Polish table have an interesting history behind them that includes a fusion of cultural influences—both foreign and regional—and most meals contain an array of grains, fresh vegetables, dumplings and noodles, rich sauces, delectable desserts, and, yes, meat and potatoes prepared in various ways, which make this cuisine truly unique.

The Middle Ages was marked by a large consumption of grains—wheat, rye, millet, groats—with meats from wild and farm animals—pigs, boars, sheep, goats, partridges, bears, and bison—herbs and local spices, and beer. Wild strawberries, blueberries, currants, blackberries, and an assortment of wild mushrooms that grow in the lush and ubiquitous forests have always been an essential part of the cuisine. Because of close trade relations Poland managed to secure with Asia, spices like pepper, nutmeg, ginger, and juniper were less expensive than in many other European countries, and flavorful sauces and aromatic dishes were a staple in many Polish households.

During the Renaissance, Bona Sforza, the Italian queen who married King Zygmunt I in the early 1500s, made her mark by introducing new vegetables like tomatoes, cauliflower, broccoli, and spinach to Polish cuisine. She also imported pasta, wine, oranges, lemons, olives, rice, figs, chestnuts, and raisins. Since then, Poles have embraced exotic and imported foods. In Poland today, there are many restaurants serving foreign cuisines like Mexican, Japanese, Chinese, French, and Italian, and many experiment with making sushi, kebabs, or pizza at home; in spite of this, most meals still feature traditional Polish fare.

Different regions of Poland have their own specialties and ways of preparing dishes. Growing up in Warsaw, I traveled to many of these regions for vacation or to visit relatives. From the most delicious fresh flounder in Gdansk, warm and sweet blueberry pierogies sold by my aunt's beach house in Jastarnia, my grandmother's traditional fluffy steamed rolls (pyzy) in Poznan, to the delectable pastries in small Krakow bakeries, oscypek (smoked and salted sheep's milk cheese) sold in roadside stalls in mountainous areas of the south, and my great-aunt's mouthwatering pâté from the meat of wild rabbits that my uncle had caught earlier in the day, my childhood memories are filled with tastes, aromas, and cravings that are only truly satisfied when I go back to my home country for a visit. Thankfully, there are now many Polish specialty stores and restaurants around the world, and those wishing for a taste of the national cuisine can have their fill.

In a time of fast food, ready-to-eat frozen meals, and processed goods, it's worthwhile to prepare a homemade meal that everyone will enjoy, and preparing a meal in Poland can be an art form. Whenever I visited either of my grandmothers as a young girl, I remember how they would begin making dinner while the rest of us were still eating breakfast. And they always planned what they would cook days in advance.

While my father's mother always (politely) asked for everyone to leave the kitchen so she could create her feasts in peace, my mother and her mother always involved the whole family in the process. From the grocery shopping, peeling, cutting, chopping, mincing, stirring (always so much stirring!) to correctly setting the table, meals with my maternal grandmother were constantly bustling.

My mother always stressed the importance of taking your time to prepare a meal correctly, and whenever I would complain that the eggs for the Easter babka didn't *have* to be beaten for so long, or that the New Year's Eve Hunter's stew could just simmer in the pot without my *having* to keep checking on it every few minutes, she would remind me that cooking requires patience for each dish to turn out perfect. And she was always right, as was proven by an undercooked babka or a burnt Hunter's stew whenever I got to do things my way.

My mother left behind scores of notebooks and binders filled with her recipes, some of which I am sharing with you in this book, as well as many old cookbooks that have inspired the rest. Whether you are of Polish descent and want to recreate your grandmother's home cooking or just want to try your hand at a new cuisine, I hope you take your time to really enjoy making these traditional soups, side dishes, meals, and desserts, and that you will share them with your family and friends for years to come.

This cookbook is dedicated to my mother—who taught me never to take shortcuts, whether cooking, baking, or going through life.

Smacznego!
Marianna Dworak

contents

SOUPS

Broths and stocks

Broth and stock are staples in Polish cuisine and are used in many dishes like soups, sauces, and fillings. Although it can be made by mixing bouillon cubes in water, a delicious broth or stock made from fresh soup vegetables is always the tastier and healthier choice.

You can use various soup vegetables, but the most common ones used are carrots, celery roots, celery stalks, onions, leeks, fresh parsley stalks, and optionally, boneless chicken.

For 2 quarts of broth:
2 carrots
½ celery root
1 celery stalk
½ onion, or scallions
1 leek
several parsley stalks
salt and pepper
optional: chicken

1. Bring 2 quarts (2 l) of water to a boil.

2. Roughly chop the carrots, celery root, celery, onion or scallions, and leek. Lower the heat of the boiling water and add in the vegetables. Add in parsley stalks at the end of cooking time. If using chicken, cut it into smaller pieces and cook for a couple of minutes before adding the vegetables.

3. Season with some salt and pepper and cook for 1–2 hours.

Broth is most often used in soups and side dishes as a base that doesn't overpower the flavor of the other ingredients.

For 2 quarts of stock:

Several bones from chicken, beef, pork, or any other animal

2 carrots

½ celery root

1 celery stalk

½ onion, or scallions

1 leek

several parsley stalks

salt and pepper

optional: chicken, or other meat pieces

1. Bring 2 quarts (2 l) of water to a boil, lower the heat and cook the bones for 2 hours.

2. Roughly chop the carrots, celery root, celery, onion or scallions, parsley stalks, and leek, and meat if you are using it, and add to the cooking stock.

3. Season with some salt and pepper and cook for 1 more hour.

Stock has a richer taste than broth and can be used to enhance the flavor of meat dishes, sauces, and gravies.

Vegetable soup

soup vegetables (2 carrots, ½ celery root, 1 leek, fresh parsley)

1 cup (100 g) cauliflower florets

½ cup (50 g) cooked corn

salt and pepper

optional: bouillon cube, onion

1. Bring 2 quarts (2 l) of water to a boil.

2. Slice the carrots, celery root, and leek into quarter-inch (6 mm) slices. Lower the heat of the boiling water and add in the sliced vegetables along with the cauliflower florets and corn. Add salt and pepper to taste, and cook on medium heat for about 40 minutes. You can optionally add a bouillon cube or some chopped onion to the soup to give it more flavor.

3. Garnish with diced parsley florets.

These are the most commonly used vegetables for the soup, but you can add in any other vegetables you like; for example, cucumbers, green peas, broccoli, etc. You can also cook this with chicken.

This soup can be poured over and enjoyed with rice or potatoes cut into half-inch (1.3 cm) cubes. You can also finely blend the soup so it has a thick consistency, mix with a couple of tablespoons of sour cream or plain yogurt to make it creamier, and add some toasted croutons.

Tomato soup

2 qt (2 l) broth
2 tbsp sour cream
1 tbsp flour
5 oz (150 ml) tomato paste
salt and pepper
dill

1. Make broth from soup vegetables (2 carrots, ½ onion, ½ celery root, 1 leek, several parsley stalks) and run it through a strainer, retaining the liquid.

2. Mix the sour cream with the flour, and add this, along with the tomato paste, to the broth.

3. Heat on the stove until it boils and add salt, pepper, and garnish with dill.

You can add rice or noodles to the soup to make it more hearty.

Pickle soup

3 potatoes

1 bouillon cube

1 tbsp butter

2 large pickles, finely diced

1 cup (250 ml) pickle juice

2 tbsp sour cream

1 tbsp flour

salt

dill

1. Peel and cut the potatoes into half-inch (1.3 cm) cubes, and boil in 2 quarts (2 l) of water along with the bouillon cube and butter.

2. After about 20 minutes, when the potatoes start to become soft, add in the finely diced pickles and the pickle juice.

3. In a separate bowl, combine sour cream and flour and gradually add in 3 tablespoons of the broth that is cooking on the stove. Then add this mixture back into the soup and boil.

4. Sprinkle in salt (but taste the soup first to see if the pickle juice isn't too strong), and garnish with some diced dill.

You can also substitute the potatoes with rice. Skip step 1, and add 3 cups of cooked rice when the soup is done.

Sour rye soup (żurek)

2 qt (2 l) broth

7 oz (200 g) kielbasa
(old country style or white),
or bacon

2 cups (500 ml) soured rye flour
(store-bought or homemade)

2 tbsp flour

Salt

2 garlic cloves

optional: mushrooms

You can buy żurek mix (soured rye flour) in a specialty store, or you can make it at home. See the recipe below.

1. Make broth by boiling soup vegetables (2 carrots, ½ onion, 1 celery, 1 leek, several parsley stalks) and the coarsely chopped kielbasa or bacon in 2 quarts (2 l) of water. Optionally, you can add in some chopped mushrooms.

2. When the vegetables are soft (after about 40 minutes), run the soup through a strainer, retaining the liquid, and add in the żurek mix and flour to the broth. You can add in some salt to taste.

3. Finely grate or dice the garlic and add in to the soup. You can serve the soup with some bacon bits or kielbasa slices.

HOMEMADE SOURED RYE FLOUR

1 cup (110 g) rye flour, or wheat flour

½ qt (½ l) of water

1. Boil half a quart of water, let it cool for a couple of minutes, and mix in rye or wheat flour. Pour the mix into a glass jar, cover with a cloth or paper towel, and leave in a warm place for 3–5 days.

Chilled beet soup (chłodnik)

1 bunch of beets

1 cucumber

3-5 radishes

dill

chives

1 qt (1 l) plain yogurt, or buttermilk

salt and pepper

sugar

optional: lemon juice

2 hardboiled eggs

1. Cut the beets from the bunch, finely dice only the stems and beet leaves, and cook them in a small amount of water until they become soft, for about 40 minutes. Set aside to cool.

2. Finely chop the cucumber, radishes, dill, and chives. Add these and the beet mix to the yogurt and mix well.

3. Add in salt, pepper, sugar, and optionally some lemon juice to taste. If you'd like a smoother texture, blend or puree the soup.

4. Serve chilled, with wedges of hardboiled eggs and diced dill.

Traditionally, only the stems and leaves of the beetroot plant are used in this soup. However, you can also use just the beets. Finely grate 1 pound of cooked beets and blend with the rest of the ingredients.

Fruit soup

1 tbsp potato flour
1 cup (250 ml) broth, chilled
2 egg yolks
3 apples
8 oz (250 g) plums,
or cherries
⅓–½ cup (75–115 g) sugar

1. Mix the flour in half of the cold broth to make a slurry.

2. In a separate bowl, mix 2 egg yolks with the remaining broth.

3. Peel the apples and plums or cherries and boil them in 1½ quarts (1½ l) of water. When they are soft, grate the fruit on a fine grater, or mix in a blender along with the water, and add some sugar to taste.

4. Mix with the flour and broth slurry.

5. Add in the egg yolk and broth mix and stir until well-combined.

You can make this soup from other fruits as well. Some popular Polish fruit soups use plums, rhubarb, wild strawberries, raspberries, blackberries, and cherries. For a milder taste, you can add in milk or sour cream and sugar.

This soup, along with the chłodnik, are perfect for hot summer months.

Strawberry soup

2 lb (900 g) fresh or frozen
strawberries

⅓ cup (75 g) sugar

optional: sour cream, noodles,
mint leaves

1. Clean and cut the strawberries into small cubes, if using fresh strawberries. Thaw the frozen strawberries for about 30 minutes.

2. Boil 2 quarts (2 l) of water, adding the sugar to dissolve. Put in three-quarters of the strawberries and boil on low heat for about 15 minutes.

3. Let the water and strawberries cool, then mix in a blender or puree until you get a smooth texture.

4. Add in the remaining strawberries and cook on low heat for about 15 minutes.

You can serve this soup hot, or leave it in the refrigerator for a couple of hours and serve chilled. You can also mix it with some sour cream, add in noodles, or decorate with mint leaves.

Vegetable barley soup (krupnik)

½ lb (225 g) meat with bone, like organ meats, chicken wings, or chicken breast

½–1 cup (110 g) barley groats or pearl barley

soup vegetables (2 carrots, ½ onion, 1 celery, 1 leek, several parsley stalks)

2 potatoes

salt and pepper

optional: sour cream, butter

1. Clean and scrape the meat and bones and boil in 2 liters of water. When the meat is soft and fully cooked, take it out of the pot, set aside to cool, slice into small pieces, and throw away the bones.

2. Rinse the barley and add to the previously made stock. Cook on low heat, stirring occasionally so that the barley does not stick to the bottom.

3. Clean, peel, and slice the soup vegetables, chop the potatoes into cubes and add to the barley and water. After about 30 minutes, when the vegetables are soft, add in sliced meat, season with salt and pepper, and optionally, add in some sour cream or butter. Garnish with some fresh parsley and serve.

Beef tripe soup (flaki)

2 lb (900 g) beef tripe,
fresh or precooked

soup vegetables (2 carrots,
½ onion, 1 celery, 1 leek,
several parsley stalks)

herbs: marjoram, basil

spices: paprika, nutmeg

salt and pepper

1 tbsp flour

1 tbsp breadcrumbs

2 tbsp butter or oil

1. Rinse and scrub the beef tripe very well in warm water, then blanch it and drain in a colander.

2. If using fresh beef tripe, cook in water for about 3 hours. If using precooked or frozen tripe, cook in water for about 20 minutes.

3. Make broth from soup vegetables. Drain the cooked tripe, place in the broth along with herbs and spices such as nutmeg, paprika, marjoram, basil, salt, and pepper, and cook for an additional 30 minutes on medium heat.

4. To make the consistency of the soup thicker, fry the flour and breadcrumbs in some butter or oil on low heat until it has some color, then mix in with the soup and cook for a couple more minutes.

You can serve the soup without vegetables, or you can slice some of the soup vegetables used for stock and add them to the soup.

Potato soup

1½ qt (1½ l) of broth

2 onions

2 leeks

5 garlic cloves

3 tbsp olive oil

4 potatoes

herbs: bay leaves, thyme, chives

salt and pepper

1. Make broth from soup vegetables and chicken, or just soup vegetables. You can also make broth with a bouillon cube.

2. Finely chop the onions, slice the leeks into quarter-inch (6 mm) rings, and fry in the olive oil, adding diced garlic cloves.

3. Clean, peel, and chop the potatoes into cubes.

4. When the onions and leeks are medium-brown, add in the potatoes, herbs, salt, and pepper. Stir for a few moments, then cover with the broth and simmer in a covered pan on low heat for about 30 minutes, until the potatoes are soft.

5. When the soup cools, blend in a blender until you get a smooth texture. Salt and pepper to taste.

Sauerkraut soup (kapuśniak)

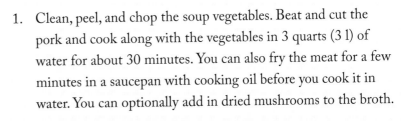

soup vegetables (2 carrots,
½ onion, 1 celery, 1 leek,
several parsley stalks)

8 oz (250 g) pork, pork ribs,
or duck

2 lb (900 g) sauerkraut

1 onion

3 tbsp cooking oil

herbs: bay leaves, thyme

salt and pepper

4 potatoes

1 cup (250 ml) sour cream

1 tbsp flour

optional: dried mushrooms

1. Clean, peel, and chop the soup vegetables. Beat and cut the pork and cook along with the vegetables in 3 quarts (3 l) of water for about 30 minutes. You can also fry the meat for a few minutes in a saucepan with cooking oil before you cook it in water. You can optionally add in dried mushrooms to the broth.

2. While the pork and vegetables are cooking, drain the sauerkraut if it contains a lot of brine or vinegar. Finely dice the sauerkraut and onion and fry in cooking oil, along with herbs, salt, and pepper on low heat until soft.

3. Clean, peel, and chop the potatoes into small cubes and add them to the soup, cooking for about 15 minutes. Then add the fried sauerkraut and cook on low heat for a few more minutes, adding salt and pepper to taste.

4. To make the soup thicker, mix the sour cream with flour and stir into the soup, additionally cooking the soup until it starts bubbling.

Lemon soup

2 qt (2 l) broth, or stock
½–1 cup (95–190 g) white rice
2 lemons
2 egg yolks
salt and pepper
optional: ½ cup sour cream

1. Make broth from 2 quarts (2 l) of water and soup vegetables (2 carrots, ½ onion, 1 celery, 1 leek, several parsley stalks) or stock.

2. In just the broth or stock liquid, cook the rice until it is soft, about 25 minutes.

3. Peel 1 lemon, slice it thinly, and add along with some salt to the cooking rice.

4. Whisk together egg yolks with the juice of the remaining lemon. You can optionally mix in sour cream with the eggs if you want a creamier soup.

5. Stir in the egg and lemon mix, constantly stirring the soup. Cook on low heat for a few minutes, adding salt and pepper to taste.

Asparagus soup

1 lb (450 g) white asparagus

soup vegetables (2 carrots, 1 leek, ½ celery root, fresh parsley)

2 tbsp butter

¼ cup (30 g) flour

salt and sugar

½ cup (125 ml) sour cream

1. Clean the asparagus, trim the ends, and peel the skins. In a pot, bring 2 quarts (2 l) of water to a boil and cook the asparagus stalks and soup vegetables until soft. Save the liquid from the broth.

2. Cook the asparagus heads separately in a small amount of water.

3. Puree the asparagus stalks, grate on a fine grater, or run through a meat grinder.

4. Mix the pureed asparagus with the broth from the soup.

5. In a skillet, fry the butter and mix in flour, stirring on low heat to make a roux. Add in to the cooking soup, along with the cooked asparagus heads, salt, and pepper. At the end stir in the sour cream and serve with croutons.

SIDES, SALADS, AND SANDWICHES

Beet salad (ćwikła)

4 beets
2 tbsp horseradish
1 tsp sugar
⅓ cup (80 ml) wine vinegar
parsley
salt and pepper

1. Clean the beets and boil in water until soft, about 30 minutes. Take them out and peel when they have cooled.

2. Grate the beets on the medium grating slots.

3. Mix the horseradish, sugar, vinegar, parsley, salt, and pepper to make a sauce, and then mix in with the beets using a fork.

4. Leave in the refrigerator for about 2 hours to cool.

You can substitute the horseradish with an onion. Lightly fry 1 diced onion in 1 tablespoon of olive oil. Mix the olive oil with the spices, then add the sauce and the onion to the beets and mix.

Sauerkraut salad

1 jar (250 g) of sauerkraut
1 apple
1 orange
⅓ cup (25 g) finely chopped walnuts
optional: onion, lemon, oil

1. Drain the sauerkraut if it has been soaked in a lot of brine.

2. Peel the apple and make a series of fine, lengthwise cuts. You can also finely chop the apple.

3. Peel and cut the orange into wedges.

4. Mix all of the ingredients, optionally adding in slices of onions and drizzling with lemon juice and/or oil.

Celery and orange salad

1 big celery root

1 orange, or 2 mandarins

⅓ cup (25 g) finely chopped walnuts

½ cup (125 ml) sour cream

salt

optional: ⅓ cup (25 g) raisins

1. Grate the celery root on the medium grating slots.

2. Peel and chop the orange or mandarins into quarter-inch (6 mm) chunks.

3. Mix the celery and oranges and walnuts, then mix in the sour cream using a fork.

Add some salt to taste. You can optionally add in some raisins.

Chicory and orange salad

3 chicory heads

2 oranges

optional: raisins

1. Wash and chop the chicory heads into small slices.

2. Peel the oranges, set aside half of an orange, and chop the remaining oranges into small cubes.

3. Mix the oranges and chicory, squeezing in orange juice from the remaining half of the orange.

Corn and cream salad

6 corn cobs (or 3 cups of
canned corn)
2 tbsp butter
½ cup (125 ml) sour cream
1 tbsp flour
parsley and dill

1. If you are using corn on the cob, trim the corn away from the cob, and boil the corn until soft.

2. Place the cooked corn on a skillet with the butter and fry for 2–3 minutes on low heat. Mix the sour cream and flour, add to the corn, and fry until it starts to boil. Then take it off the heat.

3. Garnish with parsley and dill and serve.

Pineapple and corn salad

1 celery root
½ cup (125 ml) vinegar
1 can of pineapple chunks
1 can of corn
1 apple, diced
¼ cup (60 ml) mayonnaise
¼ cup (60 ml) sour cream
½ stalk of leek

1. Roughly grate the celery and let it marinate in the vinegar for a couple of hours.

2. In a bowl, layer the grated celery, pineapple chunks, corn, and diced apple. Mix the mayonnaise with sour cream and layer on top of the salad, sprinkling the top with finely diced leeks.

You can also add a layer of ham bits.

Cucumber salad (mizeria)

1 large cucumber

⅓ cup (80 ml) sour cream, or plain yogurt

salt

1. Peel the cucumber and slice on a mandoline, or slice very thinly with a knife.

2. Mix with the sour cream and add salt to taste.

This is a very simple salad, but it is very refreshing. It goes well with any meat dish.

Vegetable and egg salad

2–3 red and yellow bell peppers

3–4 stalks of celery

5 cooked potatoes

5 hard-boiled eggs

3–4 pickles

2 scallions

1 cup mayonnaise

½ cup (125 ml) sour cream

salt and pepper

optional: tomatoes and pickle juice

1. Dice all of the vegetables and eggs into quarter-inch (6 mm) cubes and mix together.

2. Mix the mayonnaise and sour cream together, then add to the vegetables, gently stirring.

3. Salt and pepper. Optionally, you can stir in some tomatoes and pickle juice for a more tangy flavor.

Turkey garden salad

4 turkey fillets

2 oranges

2 canned peaches

4 radishes

½ onion

1 tomato

1 bag (8 oz) lettuce, or any fresh salad mix

lemon juice

olive oil

salt and pepper

1. Beat the turkey fillets with a mallet until very thin, and lightly fry them in oil. When they have cooled, cut into small squares.

2. Chop the oranges, peaches, and radishes, slice the onion and tomato, and mix with the lettuce and turkey.

3. In a small bowl, mix together some lemon juice, olive oil, salt, and pepper and pour over the salad.

Fluffy steamed rolls (pyzy drożdżowe)

1 cup (250 ml) milk, lukewarm

2 packets active dry yeast
(½ oz/14 g)

2 tsp (10 g) sugar
(½ oz/14 g)

1 lb (500 g) flour

2 eggs

2 tbsp butter, melted

1 tsp salt

1. Mix a third of the lukewarm milk with the yeast and 1 teaspoon sugar and set aside to rise for about 10 minutes.

2. In a bowl, sift flour and mix in the remaining milk, eggs, melted butter, 1 teaspoon sugar, salt, and the yeast. Knead the dough until smooth, cover with a paper towel, and set aside to rise for about 30 minutes.

3. Roll out the dough on a floured surface until it is about 1 inch (2.5 cm) thick. Cut out circles with a glass top that is about 3 inches (7.6 cm) in diameter. Cover the dough again and let rise for 20 more minutes.

4. Bring a large pot of water to a boil, place a metal sieve or steamer on top, and sparsely place the balls on top, cover, and steam for about 20 minutes.

5. When the dumplings look like fluffy balls the size of oranges, take them out and enjoy drizzled with butter, mushroom sauce, or gravy.

Meat-filled rolls (*paszteciki*)

DOUGH

1 packet active dry yeast
(¼ oz/7 g)

½ cup (125 ml) warm milk

2 cups (220 g) flour

1 cup (225 g) butter

1 egg

salt

FILLING

1 lb (500 g) meat,
like beef or pork

soup vegetables (2 carrots,
1 leek, ½ celery root, parsley)

1 onion

2 cups (200 g) mushrooms

These can be eaten with any soup, especially the Christmas beet soup on page 149.

1. Preheat the oven to 400°F (200°C).

2. Prepare the dough: Mix yeast with half of the warm milk and set aside to rise. Sift the flour and cut in butter and egg, add in the rest of the milk and salt, and knead until well-combined. Set aside to rise.

3. Prepare the filling: Cook the meat with the soup vegetables in a pot of water until soft, then take them out to cool. Dice the onion and mushrooms and lightly fry. Mince the cooked vegetables, meat, onion, and mushrooms and mix them together.

4. Roll out the dough into a rectangle a quarter-inch (6 mm) thick. Spread the filling lengthwise down the center, then fold over the two opposite sides to cover the filling. With a sharp knife, cut the roll every 2 inches (5 cm). The filling should be visible on two sides.

5. Grease a baking sheet, place the rolls on it, and bake for 20 minutes.

Cheese spreads

These are great by themselves when spread on freshly baked bread, or can be combined with other toppings on a sandwich.

HOMEMADE FARMER CHEESE

2 tbsp plain yogurt, cold

1 cup (250 ml) whole milk or skim milk

1. Mix the cold yogurt and milk.

2. Cook the liquid in a small saucepan on low heat for about 5 minutes, or until the milk starts to curdle. Make sure that it doesn't boil.

3. When you see some solids forming, take off the heat and pour the curdled milk over a very fine strainer, letting the water drain from the cheese (for a few minutes or hours, depending on how thick you want the cheese to be).

4. Place in a bowl and serve.

SANDWICH IDEA

Spread the farmer cheese on a piece of fresh bread and top with sliced tomato and sprouts.

Cucumber and radish spread

8 oz (225 g) farmer cheese

⅓ cup plain yogurt, or sour cream

½ cucumber

3–4 radishes

1 tsp (5 g) chives

1. Mix the cheese and yogurt or sour cream with a metal fork. Add in finely diced cucumber, radishes, and chives.

2. Optionally, add salt or pepper to taste, and serve.

SANDWICH IDEA

Place a generous amount of the cucumber and radish spread on a piece of bread, top with chopped tomato, and sprinkle with chives, salt, and pepper.

Onion spread (gzik)

8 oz (225 g) farmer cheese

½ cup (125 ml) plain yogurt

½ onion, minced

chives

optional: salt and pepper

1. Mix the cheese and yogurt with a metal fork. Add in the minced onion and chives.

2. Optionally, add salt or pepper to taste, and serve.

Salo spread (smalec)

1 lb (450 g) bacon

1 onion

½ apple

5–10 dried prunes

1 garlic clove

marjoram

salt and pepper

1. Cut the bacon into small pieces and fry on low heat until the fat has fully melted and the bacon bits are golden brown.

2. While the bacon is frying, finely dice the onion and finely chop the apple and prunes into small cubes, adding them to the bacon when the fat has melted.

3. Fry on low heat for a few minutes, occasionally stirring and making sure the onion and bacon don't burn. Add in minced garlic, marjoram, salt, and pepper to taste.

4. Pour the salo spread into a bowl and leave to cool and solidify. Then it can be stored in the refrigerator.

SANDWICH IDEA

Spread the salo on rye bread and garnish with pickle wedges and black olives.

Horseradish spread (chrzan)

4 horseradish roots

2 tbsp vinegar (apple or wine)

⅓ cup (80 ml) sour cream, or plain yogurt

sugar and salt

optional: 1 apple

1. Grate the peeled horseradish roots on the smallest grating slots.

2. Stir in the vinegar and sour cream or yogurt. Add a pinch of sugar and salt.

3. You can also finely grate one apple and mix it into the horseradish spread.

SANDWICH IDEA

Smear the horseradish spread on a piece of bread and garnish with pickle wedges and a piece of ham or slices of kielbasa.

Veal pâté

3 lb (1½ kg) veal (shoulder, neck, kidneys)

1 lb (500 g) bacon

2 bouillon cubes

1 lb (500 g) veal liver

2 bread rolls

3 eggs

1 onion

½ ounce (15 g) dried mushrooms

dried herbs and spices: bay leaf, thyme, nutmeg

salt and pepper

1. Clean and chop the veal and bacon and cook on low heat in a pot of water, along with the two bouillon cubes and dried mushrooms. You can optionally add in some soup vegetables, like carrots, parsley, and onion. After about 90 minutes, when the meat is soft, take it out and clean off any bones from the meat.

2. Use 1 cup of the leftover stock and sauté the liver, which has been cleaned and sliced into strips, and diced onion, on medium heat for about 10 minutes.

3. Soak the bread rolls in another cup of the leftover stock.

4. Combine the veal, liver, and bread and mix in a food processor. Mix in raw eggs, herbs, salt, and pepper.

5. Grease a loaf pan and place the meat pâté inside. It should fill about ¾ of the pan.

6. Bake in the oven at 400°F (200°C) for about 1 hour.

This meat pâté can be made from various meats like duck, rabbit, or pork.

SANDWICH IDEA
Spread the veal pâté on a piece of bread, spread some fresh cucumber slices on top, and eat with a side of the vegetable salad from page 141.

MEAT DISHES

Meat pierogies

DOUGH

3 cups (330 g) flour

1 tsp salt

1 cup warm water

FILLING

1 onion

1 lb (500 g) ground meat, like beef or veal

1 egg

salt and pepper

1 tbsp cooking oil

1. Prepare the dough: Sift the flour and mix with salt on a wooden surface. Make a hole in the middle and gradually pour in warm water and knead until a solid dough forms.

2. When the dough is smooth, roll it out into a thin sheet with a rolling pin. Cut out circles with the rim of a cup that is about 2.5 inches (6.4 cm) in diameter.

3. Chop the onion and fry in oil with the ground meat in a skillet until browned. Move the meat and onion to a bowl.

4. Beat the egg for a few minutes and add it to the meat, along with salt and pepper. If the filling is too dry, add a bit of water.

5. Place about a half-tablespoon of filling in one half of the circle, and fold over the other half to make a crescent shape. If the dough is not sticking well, moisten the edges with water before you seal them.

6. Bring a deep pot of salted water to a boil, reduce to medium heat, and put in the pierogies, about ten at a time. Stir once so they don't stick to the bottom of the pot. When they come up to the surface (after about 4 minutes), wait one more minute and take them out, one by one, with a slotted spoon.

7. If you want to make the pierogies crispy, fry them in a bit of cooking oil after taking them out of the water.

Serve sprinkled with fried bacon bits, drizzled with oil, or with a side of sour cream.

Veal with apples

1 lb (500 g) veal

2–3 sour apples, like Granny Smith

2 tbsp butter

¼ cup (30 g) flour

½ cup (125 ml) sour cream

salt

1. Rinse the veal and cook in water in a covered pot for about 30 minutes.

2. Peel and chop the apples and add them to the veal, cooking for about ten more minutes.

3. Take out the veal, pour out most of the water, and mash or blend the apples with a little bit of the remaining broth.

4. Fry the butter and flour in a skillet to make a golden roux, and add about a half-cup of water, stirring until there are no lumps. Add this to the applesauce, along with the sour cream and salt, and cook on medium heat for a couple of minutes.

5. Slice the veal into big or small pieces, and cook in the apple sauce until hot.

Serve this with groats, noodles, or kopytka (see recipe on page 82).

Walnut- and apple-stuffed pork loin

1 onion
2 apples
1¼ cup (100 g) walnuts
¼ cup (20 g) cheese, like Parmesan
1 cup (90 g) breadcrumbs
1¾ lb (800 g) pork loin without bone
dried herbs: thyme, bay leaf, oregano
¼ cup (60 ml) olive oil
½ cup (125 ml) white wine
salt and pepper

1. Preheat the oven to 425°F (220°C).

2. Chop the onion and fry it in some cooking oil until lightly brown.

3. Cut the apples into cubes and dice the walnuts.

4. Mix the apples, walnuts, shredded cheese, and breadcrumbs in a bowl, stir it into the onion, and fry for a couple of minutes on low heat. Add some herbs to taste.

5. Cut the pork loin into thick slices. Make an incision along the side of each slice to make pockets.

6. Fill each pocket with the apple and walnut mix and fasten with a toothpick or two.

7. Place the stuffed pork into a baking dish and pour the wine and olive oil over it. Sprinkle with some salt and pepper.

8. Bake in the oven for 30–40 minutes.

Stuffed pot roast

2 lb (900 g) boneless beef

salt and pepper

1 tbsp flour

2 tbsp salo (see recipe page 38), or butter

STUFFING

3 onions

1 tbsp butter

¼ cup (20 g) breadcrumbs

1 egg yolk

paprika

salt and pepper

2 tbsp flour

chopped parsley

1. Clean and lightly beat the beef then season with salt and pepper and cover with flour.

2. In a skillet with salo or butter, brown the meat on all sides then cook in a pot with 1 liter of water for 50 minutes, until the meat is tender. Don't pour out the water.

3. Prepare the stuffing: chop and fry 2 onions in butter, then add breadcrumbs, egg yolk, paprika, salt, and pepper. You can add some of the water that the meat is cooking in.

4. Take out the cooked beef and thinly slice it without cutting through to the bottom. Place the stuffing in between each of the slices then fasten the meat with metal skewers.

5. Stir in 1 tablespoon of flour to the water that the beef was previously cooked in, along with the remaining chopped onion, salt and pepper, and parsley. Place the pot roast in the pot and cook for an additional 30 minutes. The water should just cover the bottom half of the roast.

In the last 20 minutes of cooking, you can add some chopped carrots and leeks to the sauce and serve the cooked vegetables on the side.

Chicken aspic

1 lb (500 g) cooked chicken, or turkey

2 cups (500 ml) broth

½ cup (120 g) green peas

2 hardboiled eggs

2 cooked carrots

1 gelatin packet (1 tbsp)

salt and pepper

1. Use cups or a muffin pan to hold the aspic.

2. On the bottom of the cups place peas, chopped eggs, chicken slices, and sliced carrots.

3. Dissolve the gelatin in a cup of cold water, and after ten minutes mix with the broth, then stir on low heat in a saucepan until well combined.

4. Fill the cups with gelatin, covering the contents. Let stand until they solidify, then pop them out and serve on a platter lined with lettuce leaves.

Chicken de volaille

4 chicken breasts

4 tbsp butter

2 eggs

1½ cups (120 g) breadcrumbs

salt and pepper

1. Lightly pound the breast fillets with a mallet. Sprinkle salt and pepper on the thin chicken fillets.

2. Place 1 tablespoon of cold butter in the center of each fillet, fold the longer sides of the filet a quarter of the way to the center, then roll the fillet from top to bottom.

3. Lightly beat the two eggs and coat each rolled fillet in the eggs and then the breadcrumbs.

4. Heat a couple tablespoons of cooking oil on a skillet and fry the chicken de volaille until golden brown on all sides.

When you cut into the chicken roll, the butter will come gushing out. Serve with French fries and cooked vegetables.

Beef- and cabbage-stuffed croquettes (krokiety)

CREPE DOUGH

2 cups (500 ml) milk

2 eggs

4 cups (440 g) flour

salt and pepper

FILLING

1 cup (150 g) sauerkraut

1 lb (500 g) ground beef

1 onion

½ lb (250 g) mushrooms

chicken broth

salt and pepper

1. Prepare the crepe dough: In a medium bowl, whisk together milk and eggs. Gradually mix in flour, salt, and pepper. The batter should be runny; if it is too thick, add some more milk.

2. Melt 1 teaspoon of butter on a skillet on medium heat and pour in about a third cup of batter. Cook until lightly browned, and then turn over to cook the other side, until lightly browned.

3. Prepare the filling: Cook the sauerkraut in 2 cups of water for about 15 minutes until soft. For more taste, you can cook the sauerkraut in chicken broth. Drain it and put aside.

4. Peel, chop, and cook the mushrooms for about 20 minutes.

5. In a skillet, melt 1 tablespoon of butter on medium heat, add the chopped onion and ground beef, and fry until browned. Season with salt and pepper.

6. Mince the cooled sauerkraut and mix with cooked mushrooms, fried onion, and beef.

7. Place one crepe on a smooth surface and spread a third cup of the filling in the center of the crepe, leaving about a half-inch (1.3 cm) border along the edges.

8. To roll the crepe, fold two opposite corners once toward the middle, then, still pressing these corners, roll one of the two remaining corners toward the opposite end.

These stuffed crepes taste great when fried in breadcrumbs. Beat one egg in a medium bowl, dip the stuffed crepe into it, and then coat it with breadcrumbs. Heat a skillet with 4 tablespoons of cooking oil and fry on each side until golden brown.

You can leave out the ground beef and make this a vegetarian meal.

Beef- and rice-stuffed cabbage leaves

1 head of white cabbage

½ lb (500 g) ground beef

1 onion

3 cups (750 g) cooked white rice

1 egg

salt and pepper

1 qt (1 l) of broth

1. Submerge the whole cabbage head in boiling water, and cook on low heat for about 5–10 minutes. Take the cabbage out, let it cool, then carefully peel off the cabbage leaves. Put aside a couple of the outermost leaves, they will be used to cover the baking dish.

2. Prepare the filling: Fry the ground beef and diced onion in cooking oil until browned. Cook the rice and mix well with the ground beef, onion, egg, salt, and pepper.

3. Place about a quarter cup of filling in the center of each cabbage leaf, then fold two opposite sides of the leaf about 1 inch (2.5 cm) towards the center, and roll the leaf from the third side to the opposite end.

4. Grease an ovenproof baking dish, and place some single cabbage leaves on the bottom. Put in the cabbage rolls tightly side by side and completely cover with the broth, which can be made from vegetables or a bouillon cube.

5. Cover the dish and bake in the oven at 400°F (200°C) for about 1 hour and 30 minutes. You can also cook the cabbage rolls in a deep frying pan on low heat for the same amount of time.

TOMATO SAUCE

¼ cup (60 ml) cooking oil

1 tbsp flour

1 can (8 oz / 225 g) tomato paste

2 tbsp sour cream

water or broth

optional: salt, pepper, garlic, dried herbs, sugar

1. Lightly fry the oil and add in flour, mixing quickly to prevent lumps.

2. Add in the tomato paste, mixing quickly, and then the sour cream. If the sauce is too thick, add in some water or broth.

3. When you achieve a uniform color, add herbs, garlic, salt, pepper, or sugar to taste.

Meatballs in white sauce

1 lb (450 g) ground veal

1 egg

½ onion

salt and pepper

1 bouillon cube

SAUCE

2 tbsp butter

¼ cup (30 g) flour

1 cup (250 ml) broth

1 egg yolk

lemon juice, or vinegar

salt

fresh parsley

1. Mix 1 egg with the ground veal, then mix in the finely diced onion, salt, and pepper. Shape into medium-size balls.

2. In a pot, bring about half a quart (½ l) of water (just enough to cover the meatballs) to a boil. Lower the heat, put the meatballs in, add a bouillon cube, and cook for about 20 minutes.

3. Prepare the sauce: On low heat melt the butter, add in flour, and sauté until lightly brown, then add in broth (either previously made or you can use the water used for cooking the meatballs). Stir in a raw egg yolk, lemon juice or vinegar, and salt.

4. Pour the sauce over the meatballs, garnish with some chopped parsley, and serve with rice or groats.

Risoni with ground beef

4 cups (400 g) risoni pasta

1 lb (450 g) ground beef

1 onion

1 cup cooked corn

1 handful of cherry tomatoes

salt and pepper

basil

optional: 12 oz (340 g) tomato paste

1. Cook the risoni pasta according to directions on the package.

2. Dice the onion and fry in a skillet with the ground beef.

3. If using tomato paste, stir it in, then add the cooked risoni, halved cherry tomatoes, and then corn, and cook on low heat until warm. Add salt and pepper to taste and serve with chopped basil.

Chicken with white sauce and rice

1 whole chicken

4 cups cooked (900 g) cooked rice

2 carrots

1 leek

parsley

SAUCE

1 tbsp butter

2 tbsp flour

3 tbsp sour cream

stock from the chicken

1. Cook rice according to directions on the package.

2. Cook the chicken, carrots, leek, and parsley in a pot with water until soft. Save the stock.

3. In a skillet, fry the butter and mix with flour to make a roux. Then add sour cream and a couple of tablespoons of the stock, depending on how thick you want the sauce to be.

4. Cut the cooked chicken into pieces and serve with rice and the white sauce. You can chop the cooked carrots and leek and mix with the rice.

Add some raisins or pineapple chunks to the white sauce for a more tart flavor.

Kielbasa shish kabobs

13 oz (368 g) kielbasa

1 cup (125 g) white button mushrooms

1 cup (175 g) chopped red, green, and yellow bell peppers

1 onion

2 tbsp olive oil

lemon juice

pepper

1. Dice the kielbasa into half-inch (1.3 cm) thick slices.

2. Chop the bell peppers into small squares.

3. Chop the onion into small squares.

4. Mix olive oil with some lemon juice and pepper. Peel the skins off of the mushrooms, cut out the stems, and dip the mushroom caps in the oil and lemon mixture.

5. Alternate placing each ingredient on a metal skewer. Grill the kabobs for about 15 minutes, rotating every few minutes. Serve on a bed of white rice.

Coulibiac (kulebiak)

DOUGH
3 cups (330 g) flour

1 packet active dry yeast
(¼ oz/7 g)

1 tsp (5 g) sugar

½ cup (125 ml) milk

1 egg

1 egg yolk

2 tbsp butter

FILLING
1 lb (500 g) sauerkraut, or
½ cabbage head

1 oz (28 g) dried mushrooms

1 onion

2 hardboiled eggs

dried herbs: oregano, bay leaf,
caraway

salt, pepper

1 egg white

1. Prepare the dough: Mix sugar with yeast and a quarter-cup of flour and stir in lukewarm milk. Set aside in a warm area to rise.

2. After the yeast has risen, gradually add in one egg and a lightly beaten egg yolk. Add in the rest of the flour and knead, later adding melted butter and kneading until the dough is smooth. Shape into a ball, cover with a paper towel, and set aside once again to rise.

3. Prepare the filling: Soak the dried mushrooms for several hours until soft, then cook in water for about 30 minutes. If using fresh cabbage, simmer in water or broth until soft. Finely dice the cooked cabbage or sauerkraut, the cooked mushrooms, onion, and hardboiled eggs, and mix together. Add in dried herbs, salt, and pepper.

4. Separate the dough into two balls and roll out each one to half an inch (1.3 cm) thick. Grease and flour a loaf pan and cover the bottom and sides with one sheet of dough, add the filling on top, and cover with the remaining dough, making sure all of the filling is wrapped. Preheat the oven to 325°F (160°C) and set the dough aside to rise.

5. Glaze the top of the loaf with a whisked egg white and bake for about one hour.

Goulash

1 lb (450 g) meat, like veal, beef, pork, or mutton

3 tbsp flour

½ onion

soup vegetables (carrots, onion, leek, parsley, peas)

dry herbs: bay leaf, oregano, thyme

salt and pepper

1. Clean the meat and chop into small pieces. Sprinkle with 1 tablespoon of flour and cook in 2 tablespoons of oil, along with the chopped onion, in a skillet until brown.

2. Place the fried meat and onion into a pot, and cook, covered, in half-cup (120 ml) of water.

3. Dice the soup vegetables and add them along with herbs, salt, and pepper to the cooking meat after about 20 minutes. Stir occasionally and add water if too much evaporates.

4. Add in the rest of the flour to thicken the stew and bring to a boil.

Serve with rice, groats, dumplings, or potatoes.

Chicken stew

1 whole chicken (2 lb/900 g)
1 onion
1 carrot
1 celery stalk
1 tbsp flour
paprika
1 lb (450 g) bell peppers
2 tomatoes
1 cup (250 ml) broth, or water
salt
1 tbsp minced parsley

1. Cut the chicken into several smaller pieces and fry on a skillet in a couple of tablespoons of cooking oil until browned. Set aside.

2. In the same skillet, fry chopped onion, sliced or diced carrot and celery, mixing in flour and paprika. Chop the bell peppers and slice the tomatoes, and add them to the skillet along with the chicken.

3. Mix in the broth (made from soup vegetables or with a bouillon cube), add salt, and cook on medium heat until the chicken is soft and tender.

Serve on a bed of rice or potatoes, sprinkled with diced parsley.

Zucchini with ground meat

½ lb (250 g) ground meat, like beef or pork

2 zucchinis

2 carrots

2 potatoes

1 onion

1 tbsp flour

1 tbsp butter

1 egg

2 tbsp breadcrumbs

salt and pepper

2 tbsp tomato paste

1 cup (250 ml) broth

1. Clean, peel, and slice the zucchini into half-inch (1.3 cm) slices. Take out the seeds, coat with flour, and fry in butter until lightly browned on both sides.

2. Grate the carrots and potatoes on the rough grating slots, and dice the onion, mix with the ground meat, and fry in cooking oil until browned. Lightly beat the egg and mix with the fried meat and vegetables, adding salt and pepper to taste.

3. Grease an oven-proof baking dish, sprinkle the bottom with breadcrumbs, and fill with alternating layers of meat and zucchini, with a layer of zucchini on top.

4. Mix the tomato paste with broth and pour over the layers. Cook in the oven at 350°F (180°C) for about 25 minutes.

Meat- and rice-stuffed pepper

10 bell peppers

2 cups (500 g) cooked rice, white or brown

1 onion

½ lb (450 g) ground beef or pork

dry herbs: marjoram, basil parsley

salt and pepper

TOMATO SAUCE

12 oz (340 g) tomato paste

1 cup (250 ml) vegetable broth

2 tbsp flour

½ cup (120 ml) sour cream

1 tsp salt

½ tsp sugar

1. Cook the rice about half of the way through.

2. Dice and fry the onion adding the rice, ground beef or pork, marjoram, basil, parsley, salt, and pepper on the skillet.

3. Prepare the tomato sauce: In a saucepan on low heat, stir together tomato paste, vegetable broth, flour, sour cream, salt, and sugar. Let boil and take off the heat.

4. Wash the bell peppers, take out the seeds, and fill with the rice and meat mix.

5. Cover the bottom of a deep skillet with some of the tomato sauce, place the stuffed peppers on top, and cover with the rest of the sauce. Cook on medium heat until soft. If the sauce starts to become too thick, dilute with some water.

Beef stroganoff

1 lb (450 g) beef tenderloin

1-2 tbsp cooking oil

½ onion

1 cup (125 g) white button mushrooms

3 pickles

parsley

paprika

salt and pepper

⅓ cup (80 ml) sour cream

1. Clean the beef tenderloin, chop into cubes, and sprinkle with paprika, salt, and pepper. Let it marinate for 1 hour.

2. Heat the cooking oil in a skillet and fry the diced onion for a few minutes before adding the beef tenderloin.

3. After a few minutes, chop the mushrooms and add to the skillet. When the meat has browned, add in diced pickles, parsley, salt, and pepper and fry for a few more minutes on low heat.

4. At the end, stir in sour cream to make the sauce creamier.

Serve with the kluski from page 83 and mizeria from page 31.

If you want to make the sauce thicker, you can add in a tablespoon of flour when the meat has browned and stir it with the rest of the ingredients. You can also add a bit of tomato paste to the dish.

Breaded pork cutlet (kotlet schabowy)

1 lb (450 g) pork tenderloin,
or pork chop

2 eggs

½ cup (60 g) flour

1 cup (90 g) breadcrumbs

pepper

1. Clean the pork and lightly beat with a tenderizer.

2. Take out three wide bowls or plates. Pour the flour into the first dish, the beaten eggs mixed with pepper and any other spices in the second, and the breadcrumbs in the third.

3. First cover the cutlet in flour, then dredge in the egg, and lastly coat with breadcrumbs.

4. Heat oil on a skillet and fry the cutlets, turning over when golden on one side.

Enjoy with potatoes or French fries and cooked vegetables like chopped carrots and peas drizzled with melted butter.

Veal fillets in white wine

4 veal fillets

3 tbsp flour

4 garlic cloves

1 tbsp oil

paprika, rosemary, thyme

½ cup (125 ml) white wine

7 tbsp butter

2 tbsp lemon juice

1 onion

salt and pepper

1. Beat the veal fillets with a mallet until very thin and coat with flour.

2. Dice the garlic, mix with oil, paprika, rosemary, thyme, and a quarter of the white wine and coat the veal fillets with the mixture. Set aside to marinate for 1 hour.

3. In a skillet, heat up the butter, lemon juice, and the remaining white wine, and fry the diced onion, along with the veal fillets, until browned.

4. Sprinkle with salt and pepper and serve with potatoes sprinkled with parsley.

Apple-stuffed duck

1 whole duck, deboned and
thawed
lemon juice
salt and pepper
marjoram
6 apples
¼ cup (20 g) chopped walnuts
¼ cup (20 g) raisins
cooking oil

1. Sprinkle some lemon juice in the duck cavity and sprinkle salt, pepper, and marjoram on the duck.

2. Peel and chop 3 apples, mix with the walnuts and raisins, and stuff the duck. Sew the cavity with a thread or fasten with toothpicks.

3. Grease an ovenproof baking dish with cooking oil and place the duck in the oven for about 2 hours at 350°F (180°C). You will need to baste the duck with water and the melting fat to keep it from drying out.

4. In the last 20 minutes of cooking, peel and chop the remaining three apples and place them in the baking dish.

Serve with potatoes and cranberry sauce.

Sautéed liver

1 lb (450 g) beef or pork liver
1 cup (240 ml) milk
2 onions
4 tbsp butter
3 tbsp flour
2 tomatoes
salt and pepper

1. Rinse and clean the liver, cut into slices, and soak in milk for 2 hours.

2. In a skillet, fry the sliced onions in 2 tablespoons of butter until lightly brown, and set aside.

3. Add the remaining butter and fry the liver coated in flour, salt, and pepper, in the same skillet. Add the onion and sliced tomatoes at the end and sauté for a few more minutes. The liver should be brown on the outside and pink on the inside.

Serve the liver coated with the fried onion, along with potatoes and a fresh salad.

FISH DISHES

Cooked fish with dill sauce

1 lb (450 g) fish, like cod,
salmon, or trout

1 tbsp butter

salt and pepper

soup vegetables (2 carrots,
1 leek, ½ celery root, parsley)

1 onion

dried herbs: bay leaf,
oregano, thyme

DILL SAUCE
2 cups (500 ml) broth

3 tbsp minced dill

½ cup (125 ml) sour cream

1 tbsp flour

salt

1. Clean the fish, cut off the head, tail, and scales, and slice. Butter, salt, and pepper each slice.

2. Clean and chop the soup vegetables and onion. Cover the vegetables with water in a deep saucepan and cook for about 15 minutes. Then add the fish slices, sprinkle with herbs, salt, and pepper, and cook until tender, for about 15 more minutes.

3. Prepare the dill sauce: take 2 cups of the broth from the cooking fish and mix with flour, sour cream, minced dill, and salt on low heat.

Serve the fish covered in dill sauce, with the cooked soup vegetables and asparagus on the side.

Cod à la Nelson

6 cod fillets

1 oz (28 g) dried mushrooms, or fresh mushrooms

8 potatoes

3 carrots

1 onion

2 tbsp butter

½ cup (125 ml) sour cream

salt and pepper

parsley

1. If using dried mushrooms, soak overnight. Cook the mushrooms in water until soft and save the broth.

2. Peel and cook the potatoes and carrots in water, halfway through so they are not too soft. Cut into large cubes.

3. Fry the fish fillets and diced onion in butter or cooking oil.

4. Prepare the sauce: mix the sour cream with a couple tablespoons of the mushroom broth and add salt to taste.

5. Grease an ovenproof baking dish, and fill the bottom with half of the potatoes. Then layer on the codfish fillets, onion, sliced carrots, sliced mushrooms, salt, and pepper. Add another layer of potatoes and pour the sour cream and mushroom sauce on top.

6. Bake in the oven at 350°F (180°C) for about 30 minutes. Garnish with minced parsley.

Herring in cream

1 jar (32 oz/907 g)
of pickled herring

2 apples

1 onion

1½ cups (375 ml) sour cream

salt and pepper

parsley

1. Chop the herring slices into smaller pieces. Dice the apples, mince the onion.

2. Mix the sour cream with the apples, onion, salt, and pepper.

3. Mix the cream with the herrings and sprinkle with chopped parsley. Leave in the refrigerator for about 2 hours to chill.

You can substitute the apples with pickles, or add some sugar for a sweeter taste.

Trout in egg sauce

1 trout

lemon juice

salt and pepper

dried herbs: thyme, oregano

EGG SAUCE

3 tbsp butter

3 hardboiled eggs

2 tbsp minced parsley

1. Clean and gut the trout, cut off the head, tail, and gills. Cut into thick slices.

2. Coat the fish slices with lemon juice, salt and pepper, and dried herbs.

3. Wrap the fish in aluminum foil and bake in the oven on both sides for 30 minutes at 400°F (200°C).

4. Prepare the egg sauce: In a saucepan on low heat, melt the butter. Mince and add the three hardboiled eggs and stir in the parsley.

Coat the baked trout with the egg sauce and serve with some cooked sliced carrots and potatoes.

Fish in aspic

2 lb (900 g) fish (carp, northern pike, salmon, etc.)

2 gelatin packets (½ oz/14 g)

soup vegetables (or 2 onions and 2 carrots)

dried herbs: parsley, bay leaf, allspice

salt and pepper

1. Mix the gelatin in a quarter cup of cold water and set aside for 30 minutes.

2. Peel the carrots and cut them and the onions into big chunks.

3. Clean and gut the fish, and cut off the head, gills, and tail.

4. Place the soup vegetables in 1 quart (1 l) of water on high heat, and when it starts to boil, put on low heat and cook in a covered pan for 30 minutes. You can also add in the fish head and tail for more taste.

5. After 30 minutes, take out the fish head and tail if you used it for the broth. Cut the fish meat into 1-inch (2.5 cm) slices and put them back into the broth, cooking on low heat for 20 more minutes.

6. Drain the liquid from the fish and vegetables, and mix the gelatin into the broth until it completely dissolves.

7. While the broth and gelatin mix are cooling, throw out everything but the carrots and fish. Dice the carrots.

8. Put the carrots and fish slices in a bowl or glass baking dish. Then pour the slightly cooled gelatin mix covering everything. Set aside for 2 hours to stiffen.

You can garnish this dish with some egg slices and dill.

VEGETARIAN DISHES

Potato dumplings (kopytka)

1 lb (450 g) potatoes
3 cups (330 g) flour
2 eggs
salt

1. Clean, peel, and cook the potatoes until soft. Mash or puree them very well so there are no lumps.

2. On a wooden surface, mix the potatoes, sifted flour, eggs, and salt and knead into a smooth dough.

3. Split the dough into thirds, and roll out each piece with your hands into a long rope. Flatten each roll a bit by gently pressing on the top, then cut across with a knife into 1 x 1.5 inch (2.5 x 3.8 cm) pieces.

4. Drop the dumplings into a large pot of boiling salted water, about 20 at a time, cover with a lid, and then take out with a slotted spoon when they are cooked and float to the top.

These go great with any meat dishes, like meatballs, veal, or chicken. You can drizzle with melted butter or mushroom sauce (see recipe on page 155).

Dumplings (kluski kładzione)

2 cups (220 g) flour

2 eggs

½ cup (125 ml) water

salt

1. In a bowl, sift the flour and combine with 2 eggs, water, and salt. Mix vigorously using a metal spoon. The batter should be slightly runny and not too thick.

2. Bring salted water to a boil. Dip a large clean metal spoon in the boiling water for a few seconds, spoon a dollop of the dough, then dip the spoon in the water until the dumpling dough slides out. Cook about 15 dumplings for 2 minutes at a time, then take out with a slotted spoon when they float to the top.

These are often used in beef stroganoff or with any other meat dishes, and can also be put into soups like chicken noodle or vegetable.

Dumplings (łazanki)

4 cups (440 g) flour

3 eggs

½ cup (125 ml) water

salt

1. On a wooden surface, sift the flour and mix in eggs, water, and salt.

2. Shape into a smooth dough, then split into thirds, roll out each dough with your hands into a rope half an inch (1.3 cm) in diameter, and leave to dry for about half an hour.

3. Cut the rope of dough into small squares and drop into boiling salted water. Take out with a slotted spoon when the dumplings float to the top.

Serve with fried bacon bits, mixed with sauerkraut, or with meat dishes.

White cheese dumplings (kluski leniwe)

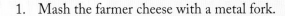

15 oz (426 g) farmer cheese
2 eggs
1 cup (110 g) flour
optional: 1 tbsp butter
salt

1. Mash the farmer cheese with a metal fork.

2. Separate the egg yolks from the egg whites. If using butter, melt it and mix with the egg yolks. Otherwise, mix the egg yolks with cheese and flour, and add a pinch of salt.

3. Beat the egg whites until fluffy and add to the dough.

4. Knead into a smooth dough and separate into thirds, rolling each dough with your hands until it is about a half-inch (1.3 cm) thick. Flatten the top gently with your hands and cut across diagonally with a knife into 1 x 1.5 inch (2.5 x 3.8 cm) pieces.

5. Bring a large pot of salted water to a boil and throw in 20 dumplings at a time, cooking for about 3 minutes until they come to the top, and take them out with a slotted spoon.

Drizzle with melted butter, sprinkle with sugar, or enjoy with yogurt or sour cream.

White cheese pancakes

DOUGH

3 eggs

3 cups (330 g) flour

3 cups (750 ml) milk

salt

FILLING

15 oz (426 g) farmer cheese

1 egg yolk

¼ cup (60 ml) sour cream,
or plain yogurt

optional: 1 tbsp powdered sugar

⅔ cup (55 g) raisins,
or chopped strawberries
or bananas

1. Separate the egg yolks from the egg whites. Whisk together egg yolks with the milk, and half of the flour.

2. Beat the egg whites until fluffy and add to the batter along with the remaining flour and salt, stirring until well-combined. If batter is too thick, add some water.

3. Heat butter on a skillet and fry about half a cup of batter at a time. When you see bubbles form on top, flip over the pancake and cook on the other side until they turn yellow.

4. Prepare the filling: mash the farmer cheese and sour cream with a metal fork, adding in the egg yolk, and stirring in sugar, and lastly raisins. When the pancakes have cooled, spread the cheese filling on half of the round pancake, fold it over, then spread some more filling on one half of the semi-circle, and fold over again to create a triangle. Sprinkle with powdered sugar and eat it cold, or warmed up in a skillet or oven.

Potato pancakes

2 lb (900 g) potatoes

1 onion

1 egg

3 tbsp flour

salt

1. Clean and peel the potatoes. Grate the potatoes and onion on the finest grating holes of a grater and mix together.

2. Add in flour, lightly beaten egg, and salt. Stir the batter until well-combined.

3. Heat cooking oil on a skillet and place about 2 tablespoons of the batter to make one pancake. Brown on both sides and serve.

These can be served salted, with a mushroom sauce or gravy, or sweet, sprinkled with granulated sugar.

Mushroom- and groat-stuffed cabbage leaves

1 head of cabbage
1.8 oz (50 g) dried mushrooms
2 onions
1 cup (150 g) buckwheat groats
2 hardboiled eggs
2 tbsp butter
parsley
salt and pepper

1. In advance, soak the dried mushrooms in cold water for about 2 hours, then cook them in the same water until they turn soft. Set the water aside and finely dice the mushrooms.

2. In a large pot, submerge the whole cabbage head in boiling water, and cook on low heat for about 5–10 minutes. Take the cabbage out, let it cool, then carefully peel off the cabbage leaves. Put aside a couple of the outermost leaves; they will be used to cover the baking dish.

3. Prepare the filling: finely dice the onions and lightly fry them with some butter. Finely dice the eggs and mix them with the mushrooms, onion, and cooked groats, adding in parsley, salt, and pepper to taste.

4. Place about a third cup of filling in the center of each cabbage leaf, then fold two opposite sides of the leaf about 1 inch (2.5 cm) towards the center, and roll the leaf from the third side to the opposite end.

5. Fill the bottom of an ovenproof baking dish with the leftover mushroom water, cover with one layer of single cabbage leaves, and place the cabbage rolls tightly side by side, adding some butter on top if desired. Place one layer of single cabbage leaves on top and cover with aluminum foil. Bake in the oven at 350°F (180°C) for about 45 minutes.

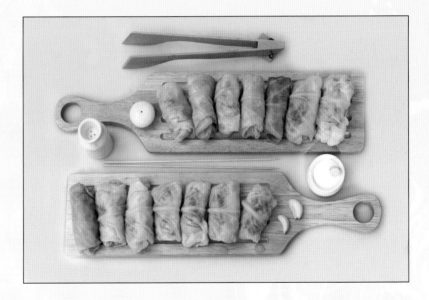

Pierogies

Making the dough for pierogies is very simple, but there are several ways to do it. Here are three ways that will yield about 40 pierogies:

3 cups (330 g) flour

1 tsp (5 g) salt

1 cup (250 ml) warm water

1. Sift the flour and mix with salt on a wooden surface. Make a hole in the middle and gradually pour in warm water and knead until a solid dough forms.

3 cups (330 g) flour
1 tsp (5 g) salt
1 cup (250 ml) warm water
2 tbsp butter

1. Sift the flour into a bowl and mix with salt.

2. Boil the water, let it cool a little bit, then melt the butter in the warm water.

3. Gradually pour the water into the flour, kneading with your hands, adding flour if the dough is too sticky.

3 cups (330 g) flour
1 tsp (5 g) salt
1 egg
warm water

1. Sift the flour and mix with salt on a wooden surface, scooping some out from the center to make a hole.

2. Break the egg into the hole and mix with a fork. Gradually add in water and knead with your hands until the dough is not too sticky and not too dry.

When the dough is smooth, roll it out with a rolling pin into a thin sheet. Cut out circles with the rim of a cup that is about 2.5 inches (6.4 cm) in diameter. Place about 1 tablespoon of filling in one half of the circle, and fold over the other half to make a crescent shape. If the dough is not sticking well, moisten the edges with water before you seal them.

Bring a deep pot of salted water to a boil, reduce to medium heat, and put in the pierogies, about ten at a time. Stir once so they don't stick to the bottom of the pot. When they come up to the surface (after about 4 minutes), wait one more minute and take them out, one by one, with a slotted spoon.

If you want to make the pierogies crispy, fry them in a bit of cooking oil after taking them out of the water.

You can drizzle the pierogies with melted butter or olive oil.

Potato pierogies (ruskie)

2 lb (900 g) potatoes
1 onion
8 oz (225 g) farmer cheese
1 tbsp butter, or oil
salt and pepper

1. Peel and cook the potatoes until soft.

2. Chop and lightly fry the onion.

3. Mix the potatoes, onion, and farmer cheese and mash or grind in a food processor. Add salt and pepper to taste and a little bit of oil or butter to moisten the filling.

4. Fill each pierogi with about 1 tablespoon of the potato filling, seal, place in a pot of boiling water, and cook until the pierogies float to the top.

Drizzle with oil or melted butter, and serve with fried bacon bits.

Fruit pierogies

*1 lb (450 g) fresh fruit
like blueberries, strawberries,
cherries, or bilberries*

1. Wash the fruit. If using larger fruit, like strawberries or cherries, chop them into smaller pieces.

2. Fill each pierogi with about 1 tablespoon of the fruit, seal, add to boiling water, and cook until the pirerogies float to the top.

Drizzle with melted butter, sprinkle with some sugar, or mix sour cream or plain yogurt with sugar and pour over the pierogies.

Farmer cheese pierogies

15 oz (426 g) farmer cheese

2 egg yolks

⅓ cup (75 g) sugar

1 pinch vanilla sugar

optional: fresh fruit, like strawberries or blueberries

1. Mash the farmer cheese with a fork, or run through a meat grinder.

2. Mix the cheese with egg yolks, sugar, and add vanilla sugar to taste. You can just use the cheese as filling or mix in some fresh chopped fruit.

3. Fill each pierogi with about 1 tablespoon of the cheese filling, place in a pot of boiling water, and cook until the pierogies float to the top.

Serve with sour cream and sugar or sprinkle with cinnamon.

Plum dumplings (knedle)

1 lb (450 g) potatoes

1 cup (110 g) wheat flour, or all-purpose flour

1 egg

salt

1 lb (450 g) fresh damson plums

1. Peel and cook the potatoes until soft. Mash or puree in a food processor when they have cooled, making sure no lumps remain.

2. Mix the potatoes with flour, egg, and salt and roll out into a very thin sheet of dough.

3. Clean and pit the plums.

4. Cut the dough into circles 1.5 inch (3.8 cm) in diameter and completely cover each plum with the thin dough.

5. Drop a couple of the dumplings into a pot of boiling salted water, stir to make sure they don't stick to the bottom, and cook covered until they float to the top. Uncover the pot and let them cook for 3–4 more minutes, then take them out with a slotted spoon.

You can also make the dough without potatoes:

4 cups (440 g) flour
2 tbsp butter
1 egg
water
salt

1. Sift the flour onto a wooden surface, and mix with butter, egg, and salt. Add some water if it is too thick and knead into a soft dough.

2. Roll out into a thin sheet and cover the plums, or other fruit like strawberries or apples.

Serve drizzle with melted butter and sprinkled with sugar.

Rice with fruit

2 cups (450 g) white rice, or brown rice

fresh fruit like strawberries, cherries, blueberries, pineapple, bananas, or plums

sour cream, or plain yogurt

sugar

1. Cook the rice until soft.

2. Clean the fruits. If using bigger fruit, like strawberries, pineapple, bananas, or plums, chop them into smaller pieces.

3. Place the fruit on a bed of rice, drizzle with sour cream or yogurt, and sprinkle with sugar.

You can also make this rice with cooked apples:

1 lb (450 g) of apples

2 egg whites

1 tbsp powdered sugar

cinnamon

sugar

sour cream, or plain yogurt

1. Cook the rice until soft and place in a baking dish.

2. Clean, peel, and cut the apples into quarters and place them on the rice. Sprinkle with some cinnamon and sugar.

3. Beat two egg whites, mixing them with powdered sugar, until stiff peaks form. Spread them over the rice and apples.

4. Bake in the oven at 350°F (180°C) for about 15–20 minutes.

Enjoy with sour cream or yogurt.

Baked apples in flaky dough

1⅓ cup (250 g) flour, all-purpose or whole-wheat flour

⅔ cup (150 g) butter

1 tbsp sour cream, or white wine

2 tbsp sugar

2 lb (900 g) apples

cinnamon

1. Preheat the oven to 350°F (180°C).

2. Prepare the dough: Sift the flour and cut in butter, adding in sour cream or white wine and sugar. Knead until the dough is well-combined. Set aside for 1 hour.

3. Peel the apples and sprinkle with cinnamon.

4. Roll out the dough thinly and cut out squares and small circles. Place an apple in a dough square, pinch the four corners together around the apple, then cover the top with the dough circle.

5. Bake in the oven for 30–45 minutes. You can check if the apples are done by piercing them with a fork; they should be tender.

CAKES
AND
DESSERTS

Angel wings (chrust)

2 cups (220 g) flour

3 egg yolks

½ cup (125 ml) sour cream

1 tsp (5 ml) distilled alcohol, or distilled vinegar

1 cup (250 ml) cooking oil

optional: 1 tsp (7 g) baking powder, vanilla extract

1. On a wooden surface, sift the flour and mix with baking powder, egg yolks, sour cream, vanilla extract, and alcohol.

2. Roll out into a very thin sheet of dough and cut out into 1 x 6 inch (2.5 x 15 cm) rectangles. Make a 2-inch (5 cm) slit lengthwise in the center of each strip of dough. Take one side of the dough and thread it once through the opening. Sprinkle all of the strips with flour.

3. Heat the cooking oil until very hot in a deep skillet. Place each strip in the oil and fry, turning them quickly with a metal fork, until golden on all sides.

4. Place the hot angel wings on a plate covered with paper towels to soak up excess oil.

When they have cooled, sprinkle with powdered sugar.

Polish doughnuts (pączki)

2 packets active dry yeast
(½ oz/14 g)

1½ cups (375) milk

5 cups (550 g) flour

½ cup (50 g) sugar

7 egg yolks

vanilla extract

2 tbsp distilled alcohol

lemon peel, or orange peel

½ cup (115 g) butter

marmalade or jam: rose, cherry,
or strawberry

2 cups (500 ml) of cooking oil

1. With a wooden spoon, mix the yeast with half-cup of warm milk and stir in 1 tablespoon of flour and 1 teaspoon of sugar. Cover with a paper towel and set aside in a warm place to rise.

2. Mix the egg yolks, remaining sugar, and vanilla extract and beat until white and fluffy.

3. Sift the remaining flour and mix with risen yeast, beaten eggs, alcohol, and grated lemon peel, adding the remaining warm milk to make dough that is not too sticky or runny, and not too thick. Mix in the melted butter at the end, and knead until the dough is springy and smooth. Cover with a paper towel and set aside in a warm area to double in size.

4. When the dough has risen, form it into small pancakes, add a teaspoon of marmalade or jam in the middle, and shape the dough into a ball. Cover the doughnuts and let them rise for about 10 minutes.

5. Heat the cooking oil in a deep skillet until very hot. Place a doughnut in the oil, and cook covered. When the bottom starts to brown, turn the doughnut over and cook covered until it is brown on the top and bottom, with a white ring around the center.

6. Take out the doughnuts and wipe off excess oil with a paper towel.

When the doughnuts have cooled, sprinkle with powdered sugar or glaze with icing made from powdered sugar and lemon juice.

Cream puffs (ptyś)

3 tbsp butter
1½ cups (170 g) flour
4 eggs
salt

1. Preheat the oven to 350°F (180°C).

2. In a saucepan, bring 1 cup (250 ml) of salted water and butter to a boil, mixing it well. On medium heat, sift the flour into the water and briskly mix with a wooden spoon, making sure no lumps form.

3. When the batter is smooth and shiny, take the saucepan off the heat, let it cool for a few minutes, then stir in one egg at a time until the batter is well-combined.

4. Grease a metal baking sheet, scoop out dollops of the batter the size of lemons with a metal spoon, and place on the baking sheet.

5. Bake in the oven for 25 minutes. Be sure not to open the oven too early or the puffs may collapse. They are ready when they are hard, dry, and golden.

You can cut these in half with a sharp knife and fill them with ice cream or cream. To make cream, beat whipping cream with an electric mixer, adding in powdered sugar, vanilla extract, fruit syrup, or a couple drops of lemon juice. You can also mix in some raisins.

This dough can be also used for éclairs. Instead of shaping them into balls, shape the batter into logs on the metal baking sheet and bake for the same amount of time. Then fill with whipped cream and drizzle melted chocolate on top.

Mazurek cake with chocolate and dried fruit topping

DOUGH

5 cups (550 g) flour

1½ (170 g) powdered sugar

1 cup (225 g) margarine

2 egg yolks

1 whole egg

2 tbsp sour cream

1 tsp baking powder

FILLING

2 gelatin packets (½ oz/14 g)

1 cup (250 ml) sour cream

1 cup (225 g) sugar

2 tbsp cocoa powder

2 cups (160 g) bakalie (see page 109)

2 egg whites

1. Preheat the oven to 350°F (180°C).

2. Prepare the dough: On a wooden surface, mix the flour and powdered sugar, and cut in margarine. Add in egg yolks and whole egg, sour cream, and baking powder.

3. Knead the dough until smooth, then separate into two balls, and roll out each one with a rolling pin until they are about 1 inch (1.5 cm) thick.

4. Bake each dough separately in a 8 x 12 inch (20 x 30 cm) rectangular cake pan for 20 minutes.

5. Prepare the filling: Mix two packets of gelatin in warm water. Mix the sour cream, sugar, and cocoa powder in a saucepan, and cook on low heat for 10 minutes. You can add some vanilla extract for a nice aroma.

6. Turn off the heat and add in the *bakalie* and gelatin. Set aside to cool.

7. Beat the egg whites for a few minutes and stir the fluffy foam into the sour cream and *bakalie* mix. If the filling is too sweet, add some lemon juice.

8. When the mixture has a thick consistency, spread it inbetween the two cake shells.

9. You can serve as is, or bake in the oven for 15 more minutes at 400°F (200°C).

You can decorate the cake with chopped almonds, sprinkle the cake with powdered sugar, or glaze with icing.

Bakalie is a fruit and nut mix that is used in cakes, with muesli, and desserts. To make it, dice walnuts, dried figs, dried apricots, dried plums, and candied orange or lemon peel. Mix these along with raisins.

When mixing with dough for a cake, sprinkle the *bakalie* with a bit of flour first, and then mix into the dough batter using a wooden spoon.

Flaky mazurek dough

DOUGH

4 cups (440 g) flour, all-purpose
or wheat flour

1 cup (110 g) powdered sugar

½ tsp (3 g) baking powder

¾ cup (170 g) butter

3 hardboiled eggs

1. On a wooden surface, combine sifted flour, sugar, and baking powder, and using a knife, cut in the butter.

2. Use only the egg yolks from the hardboiled eggs. Grate the egg yolks on a fine grater and mix into the flour mix.

3. Knead the dough until well-combined. If it is too thick or dry, add in some milk. Chill the dough in the refrigerator for about 30 minutes. Preheat the oven to 350°F (180°C).

4. Grease a 12 x 16 inch (30 x 40 cm) metal baking sheet. Roll out the chilled dough (it should be ⅓ inch/8 mm thick), and place on the metal sheet.

5. Bake in the oven for about 25 minutes, until golden.

4 cups (440 g) flour,
all-purpose or wheat flour

½ cup (115 g) sugar

½ tsp (3 g) baking powder

¾ cup (170 g) butter

4 egg yolks

There is an alternate way to make this flaky dough:

1. On a wooden surface, sift the flour and mix with sugar and baking powder. With a knife, cut in the butter and add egg yolks.

2. Quickly knead the dough until smooth, adding milk if the dough is too thick or dry.

3. Chill in the refrigerator for 30 minutes and bake on a greased metal baking sheet for 25 minutes at 350°F (180°C).

You can top the baked mazurek cake with a chocolate or orange glaze, or combine them as shown in the picture.

CHOCOLATE GLAZE

⅓ cup (75 g) butter
⅓ cup (40 g) cocoa powder
⅓ cup (80 ml) milk
1 cup (225 g) sugar
optional: vanilla extract

1. In a small saucepan melt the butter on low heat. While stirring, add in cocoa powder, milk, sugar, and optional vanilla extract. Stir on low heat for a couple of minutes until it boils and the ingredients are well-combined.

2. After the mazurek cake has cooled, spread the chocolate on top and let it harden.

ORANGE GLAZE

2 lemons

4 oranges

2 cups (450 g) sugar

1. Clean and cut the lemons and oranges, take out the seeds, and puree the pulp and peels in a food processor or grate on the smallest slots of a grater.

2. Stir in sugar and mix well.

3. In a saucepan, bring half a cup of water to a boil, turn to low heat, mix in the orange and sugar mass, and let it simmer for about 30 minutes, stirring occasionally. You can also mix in some dissolved gelatin.

4. Let the mass cool, then pour it over the baked cake and let it stiffen.

Sponge cake with fruit and cream

DOUGH
4 eggs
1 cup (110 g) powdered sugar
1 cup (110 g) flour
1 tsp (5 g) baking powder

FILLING
½ cup (125 ml) whipping cream
2 tbsp powdered sugar
vanilla extract, or lemon juice
fresh fruit, like strawberries,
bananas, kiwis, or peaches

1. Preheat the oven to 350°F (180°C) and grease a round cake pan with a 9-inch (23 cm) diameter.

2. Prepare the sponge cake: separate the egg whites from the yolks, and beat the egg whites with ⅓ cup of powdered sugar until stiff peaks form.

3. Stir in the egg yolks, flour, remaining sugar, and baking powder into the beaten egg whites.

4. Pour the batter into the greased cake pan and bake for about 25 minutes.

5. Let the cake cool, then cut it into three thinner cakes using a sharp knife.

6. Make the filling: Using an electric mixer, whip the cream with the powdered sugar until soft and creamy. Add in some vanilla extract or lemon juice.

7. Place one layer of the sponge cake at the bottom of the cake pan and spread half of the whipped cream and chopped fresh fruit on top. Cover with the second layer and spread the remaining half of whipped cream and fresh fruit on top. Cover with the remaining layer of cake and decorate with fresh fruit.

8. Chill in the refrigerator for at least 1 hour before serving.

To give the sponge cake even more flavor, you can soak the middle layer of cake in fruit syrup or liquid gelatin.

Jam-filled crescent rolls

5 cups (550 g) flour

1 cup (225 g) butter

3 egg yolks

1 cup (250 ml) sour cream, or
½ cup (125 ml) heavy cream

1 packet active dry yeast
(¼ oz/7 g)

1 tbsp sugar

Jam, any flavor

optional: 1 egg white

1. Preheat the oven to 400°F (200°C).

2. Sift the flour, and knead together all of the ingredients, except the jam. Roll out the dough and cut out triangles, about 4 inches (10 cm) long and 2 inches (5 cm) wide at the bottom.

3. Place a dollop of jam at the base of each triangle, and roll to make a crescent. You can glaze the dough with an egg white and sprinkle coarse sugar on top.

4. Bake on a greased baking sheet for 30 minutes, until golden.

A great filling to use for these rolls is rose petal jam, which you can make at home. In Poland, dog rose is used, but you can use the petals of any wild roses that are free of pesticides.

¼ lb (120 g) rose petals

1 cup sugar

1 lemon

1. Rinse the petals thoroughly, Cut out the white parts, and boil in 1 quart (1 l) of water for 5 minutes. Drain the water.

2. Using a mortar and pestle, mash the rose petals, adding in sugar and juice from 1 lemon. You can also use a hand mixer and mix until the juice comes out.

3. When the jam solidifies and the sugar fully dissolves in the mixture, place the jam in a jar and store in a cool place.

Banana and Jell-O layer cake

sponge cake

LAYER 1
1 cup (225 g) butter

¾ cup (85 g) powdered sugar

3 egg yolks

6–7 bananas

2 Jell-O packs, peach or gooseberry flavor

LAYER 2
2 Jell-O packs, wild strawberry or strawberry flavor, mixed with half the amount of water to make it more concentrated

3 egg whites

LAYER 3
2 Jell-O packs, orange or lemon flavor

1. Prepare the sponge cake using a third of the recipe on page 114 and place at the bottom of a round cake pan.

2. Prepare layer 1: Mix the softened butter and sugar with an electric whisk. Gradually add in egg yolks and mashed bananas and keep mixing until the batter is smooth.

3. Add in slightly watery Jell-O (let it stand for half the time that it says on the package), and mix with a wooden spoon, until well-combined.

4. Place this layer on top of the sponge cake.

5. Prepare layer 2: Mix Jell-O with half of the water contents as recommend on the package, to make the flavor stronger. Beat the egg whites until fluffy and mix with the slightly watery Jell-O.

6. Place this layer on top of the first layer. You can add in some sliced fruit on top, like bananas, strawberries, kiwi, etc.

7. Prepare layer 3: Pour the slightly watery orange or lemon Jell-O on top of the second layer.

8. Chill in the refrigerator until the mass solidifies, for about 1 hour.

Shortbread cookies with cream

COOKIES
2 cups (220 g) wheat flour
1 tsp (5 g) baking powder
¼ cup (50 g) ground walnuts
2 hardboiled egg yolks
½ cup (115 g) butter
¼ cup (60 ml) sour cream
½ cup (60 g) powdered sugar

CREAM
chocolate pudding
1 packet gelatin (1 tbsp)
1 cup (225 g) butter
⅓ cup (80 ml) sour cream

1. Prepare the cookies: Mix the flour, baking powder, ground walnuts, and finely chopped egg yolks.

2. Add in butter, sour cream, and sugar, and knead the dough.

3. Chill in the refrigerator for 30 minutes.

4. Take out the dough and roll it out with a rolling pin until the sheet of dough is about a quarter-inch (5 mm) thick. Cut out shapes with a cookie cutter and bake on a parchment-covered baking pan at 350°F (180°C) for 15 minutes.

5. Prepare the cream: Make the pudding following the instructions on the package. Mix it with the gelatin and after it cools for a bit, add in the butter and sour cream. Chill in the refrigerator for a couple of minutes.

6. Put the filling in between two cookies and enjoy!

White cheese cookies

8 oz (225 g) farmer cheese

1⅔ cups (150 g) flour

⅔ cup (150 g) margarine

1 egg yolk

1 pinch vanilla sugar

1 egg white

powdered sugar

1. Preheat the oven to 325°F (160°C).

2. Mash the cheese with a fork and place on a wooden board.

3. Add the flour, margarine, and egg yolk to the cheese and knead the dough with your hands until smooth. Place in the refrigerator for 2–3 hours.

4. Roll out the chilled dough with a rolling pin into a thin sheet.

5. Cut out shapes with a cookie cutter and place the cookies on a flour-covered baking pan. Brush the cookies with egg whites.

6. Bake in the oven for 6–8 minutes, until they turn yellow.

7. Sprinkle with powdered sugar.

Shortbread cookies

2 cups (220 g) flour
½ cup (115 g) margarine
1 pinch vanilla sugar
1 tbsp sour cream
butter for greasing

1. Mix all of the ingredients and place the dough in the refrigerator for about one hour.

2. Roll out the chilled dough with a rolling pin until very thin and cut out shapes with a cookie cutter.

3. Place the cookies on a buttered baking pan and bake in the oven at 325°F (160°C) for 15 minutes.

4. If you like, you can glaze the cookies with egg whites and sprinkle with sugar before baking, or sprinkle with powdered sugar after baking.

These taste great with jam!

Cream cake (karpatka)

DOUGH

1 cup water

1 cup (225 g) margarine, or butter

1 cup (110 g) flour

6 eggs

FILLING

2 cups (½ l) milk

3 tbsp flour

1 pinch vanilla sugar

½ cup (115 g) butter

1 cup (225 g) sugar

1 egg yolk

1. Preheat the oven to 400°F (200°C).

2. Prepare the dough: Boil water and margarine until well-combined, stir in flour, and cook on low heat for a few minutes, making sure no lumps form.

3. When the mass has cooled, mix in one egg at a time with an electric mixer. Divide the batter in two and bake until the dough is golden, about 15–20 minutes. Set aside.

4. Prepare the filling: Cook the milk on low heat, and stir in flour and some vanilla sugar. When the mixture is thick like pudding, set aside to cool. Using an electric mixer, mix together the butter, sugar, and egg yolk until well-combined. Then mix in the milk mixture, 1 tablespoon at a time.

5. Spread the filling between the two cakes, sprinkle with powdered sugar, and serve.

Walnut cake

DOUGH

5 cups (550 g) flour

2 eggs

1 cup (225 g) sugar

1 tsp baking soda

½ cup (125 ml) honey

FILLING

1 cup (250 ml) milk

1¼ cups (250 g) finely ground walnuts

½ cup (115 g) butter

2 eggs

1½ cups (340 g) sugar

CHOCOLATE CREAM

½ cup (115 g) butter

½ cup (60 g) powdered sugar

2 tbsp water

2 tbsp cocoa powder

2 tsp distilled alcohol, or liquor

1. Preheat the oven to 350°F (180°C).

2. Prepare the dough: Sift the flour and knead together all of the ingredients for the dough. Divide into three balls, roll out, grease three round cake pans, and bake for about 20 minutes.

3. Prepare the filling: Boil a cup of milk and pour over the ground walnuts, then drain away the milk. In a bowl, mash the softened butter with a mallet. In a saucepan on low heat, beat the eggs, gradually adding the sugar, until a thick and fluffy mass forms. Take off the heat and continue beating until the mass cools, then gradually beat into the butter. At the end, mix in the walnuts.

4. Spread the filling between the three layers of cake.

5. Prepare the chocolate cream: In a saucepan, melt the butter on low heat and stir in sugar, cocoa powder, water, and alcohol.

Spread the chocolate cream around the cake and decorate with walnuts and raisins.

Walnut log

DOUGH

1 packet active dry yeast
(¼ oz/7 g)

⅓ cup (80 ml) milk

1 tbsp sugar

3 cups (330 g) flour

½ cup (115 g) margarine, or
butter

3 egg yolks

1 tbsp sour cream

WALNUT FILLING

1 cup (250 ml) milk

1¼ cups (250 g) finely
ground walnuts

½ cup (115 g) butter

2 eggs

1½ cups (340 g) sugar

1. Prepare the dough: Dissolve the yeast with 1 teaspoon of sugar in a third cup of warm milk and set aside to rise.

2. On a wooden surface, sift the flour and cut in cold margarine. Mix in yeast, egg yolks, remaining sugar, and sour cream and knead the dough.

3. Prepare the filling: Boil a cup of milk and pour over the ground walnuts, then drain away the milk. In a bowl, mash the softened butter with a mallet. In a saucepan on low heat, beat the eggs, gradually adding the sugar, until a thick and fluffy mass forms. Take off the heat and continue beating until the mass cools, then gradually beat into the butter. At the end, stir in the walnuts.

4. Roll out the dough into a rectangle that is quarter-inch (6 mm) thick. Spread the walnut filling leaving an inch-long (2.5 cm) border around the edges. Roll the dough lengthwise and close up the other two sides.

5. Place the log in the refrigerator for 30 minutes and preheat the oven to 375°F (190°C). Bake for about 1 hour.

You can also make the walnut filling following the recipe on page 123.

Cheesecake with chocolate dough

DOUGH

4 cups (440 g) flour

1 tsp baking powder

1⅓ cups (300 g) margarine, or butter

2½ cups (270 g) powdered sugar

½ cup (60 g) cocoa powder

3 egg yolks

3 tbsp sour cream

CHEESE FILLING

1 packet of vanilla or cream pudding

4 eggs

1¾ cups (395 g) sugar

⅔ cup (150 g) butter

32 oz (900 g) farmer cheese

1. Preheat the oven to 350°F (180°C).

2. Prepare the dough: Mix flour and baking powder on a wooden surface. Using a knife, cut in cold margarine or butter, then add sugar, cocoa powder, egg yolks, and sour cream.

3. Knead the dough into a ball and place it in the refrigerator for about 30 minutes to chill.

4. Prepare the cheese filling: Make the pudding in advance, following the directions on the package. Mix the eggs, sugar, and butter with an electric mixer and stir in pudding and cheese with a wooden spoon.

5. Prepare the meringue: beat the egg whites in a bowl submerged in warm water, then gradually add sugar while still beating. The meringue is ready when stiff peaks form.

6. Separate the dough into two balls and roll out each one. Add the filling inbetween the two cakes and spread the meringue on top. You can bake this cheesecake in a round cake pan or a rectangular baking sheet.

MERINGUE

2 egg whites

1¾ cups (195 g) superfine sugar

7. Bake in the oven for about 1 hour.

Adding some chopped fruit on top, like pears or peaches, makes this cheesecake even more delicious.

Apple pie (szarlotka)

4 cups (440 g) flour
1 tsp baking powder
¾ cup (170 g) margarine, or butter
2 eggs
¾ cup (170 g) sugar
optional: 2 tbsp sour cream
10 green apples

1. Preheat the oven to 350°F (180°C).

2. On a wooden surface, sift the flour, mix in baking powder, and cut in cold margarine. Add in the eggs, sugar, and optionally, sour cream. Wrap half of the dough in plastic foil and place in the freezer to harden.

3. Roll out the other half of the dough and place in a greased pie dish.

4. Prepare the apples: You can either grate the apples with the peel on the rough side of a grater, or peel the apples and chop into quarters. Place the apples on the dough in the pie dish.

5. Take out the hardened dough from the freezer and using rough grating slots cover the apples with the flaked dough.

6. Bake in the oven for 45 minutes. When the pie has cooled, top with icing made from mixing lemon juice and powdered sugar.

Walnut crescent cookies

1⅓ cups (150 g) flour
6 tbsp butter
⅓ cup (65 g) finely ground walnuts
¼ cup (55 g) sugar

1. Preheat the oven to 300°F (150°C).

2. Combine all of the ingredients and knead into a dough.

3. With your hands, roll out the dough to form a long rope and cut it every 3 inches (7.5 cm).

4. Shape each piece into a crescent and place on a baking sheet.

5. Bake in the oven for about 20 minutes, until the cookies start to brown lightly. Let cool and sprinkle with powdered sugar.

Pear chocolate cake (murzynek)

1 cup (225 g) margarine, or butter

1½ cups (340 g) sugar

1 cup (250 ml) water

3 tbsp cocoa powder

vanilla extract

2 cups (220 g) flour

2 tsp baking powder

4 egg yolks

4 egg whites

2–3 pears, fresh or canned

1. Preheat the oven to 350°F (180°C).

2. In a saucepan on low heat, combine the margarine, sugar, water, cocoa powder, and vanilla extract, stirring with a wooden spoon until the sugar melts and the ingredients are well-combined.

3. Let the mixture cool. Add in the flour, baking powder, 4 egg yolks (one at a time), beaten egg whites, and stir with a wooden spoon.

4. Grease a loaf pan and pour the batter about ¾ to the top. Place the peeled pear wedges on top of the cake, pressing slightly so they are half submerged.

5. Bake in the oven for 35–40 minutes.

Alternately, you can make icing from the mixture prepared in step 2. Set aside a third of the mixture and follow the rest of the directions. After baking the cake, drizzle the icing on top.

Crumbly yeast cake (ciasto drożdżowe)

2 packets active dry yeast
(½ oz/14 g)
½ cup (125 ml) milk
1½ cups (340 g) sugar
4 cups (440 g) flour
4 eggs
1 cup (225 g) butter
1 pinch vanilla sugar
salt

CRUMBLE
2 cups (220 g) flour
½ cup (115 g) sugar
½ cup (115 g) butter
optional: bakalie, nuts,
sliced fruit

1. Preheat the oven to 350°F (180°C).

2. Mix the yeast and 1 tablespoon of sugar in the warm milk and let stand for 10 minutes.

3. In a bowl, combine the dissolved yeast, flour, eggs, melted butter, vanilla sugar, and salt. The batter should be thick but not stiff.

4. Pour the batter into a clean kitchen rag, and tie the top. Place it in a big bowl filled with cold water and wait until it floats to the top.

5. Pour the batter back into a bowl, mix with the remaining sugar, cover with a paper towel, and set aside in a warm place for 1 hour.

6. Prepare the crumble: Mix the flour and sugar in a bowl. Stir in the hot melted butter and mix with your hands until you get a crumbly mixture.

7. Pour the risen dough into a greased baking pan and sprinkle the crumble on top.

8. Optionally, you can place bakalie (see recipe on page 109), nuts, or some sliced fruit on top, like peaches, apples, pears, or plums.

9. Place in the oven and bake for about 45 minutes.

You can sprinkle with powdered sugar and enjoy with a warm glass of milk.

Plum stew (powidła)

2 lb (900 g) fresh plums
optional: ¾ cup (170 g) sugar

1. Rinse and pit the plums.

2. Boil the plums in a small amount of water (the water should just cover them), stirring occasionally. After about two hours, sugar can be added for a sweeter taste.

3. When most of the water has evaporated and the stew is thick, pour into glass jars and store in a cool place.

For more flavor, you can stir in nutmeg, lemon juice, or cinnamon near the end of cooking time.

Marmalade

2 lb (900 g) fresh fruit,
like apples, pears, apricots,
cherries, and/or strawberries

1¾ cups (395 g) sugar

1. Clean, peel, and pit the fruit or fruits, depending on which you use.

2. Boil in a small amount of water (the water should just cover them), stirring occasionally.

3. When the fruit is soft, puree in a blender or grate on the smallest grating holes.

4. Cook on low heat, stirring in sugar, until the mass is thick.

5. Pour into glass jars and store in a cool place.

Jam

2 lb (900 g) fresh fruit, like strawberries, raspberries, cherries, and/or blueberries.

2 cups (450 g) sugar

1. Clean, peel, pit, and chop the fruit or fruits, depending on which you use.

2. Mash half of the fruit, mix with sugar, and set aside to marinate for about 2 hours.

3. Cook on low heat in a saucepan. When the mixture starts to thicken, add in the rest of the chopped fruit and stir occasionally.

4. When the jam is thick, pour into glass jars and store in a cool place.

Enjoy the plum stew, marmalade, or jam on bread or use as filling in cookies or Polish doughnuts (on page 103).

HOLIDAYS

Easter Rabbit meat pâté

2 lb (900 g) rabbit meat
1 lb (450 g) pork
2 oz (60 g) bacon
2 bouillon cubes
1 lb (450 g) veal liver
2 bread rolls
3 eggs
dry herbs and spices: bay leaf, thyme, nutmeg
salt and pepper
optional: soup vegetables

1. Clean and chop the rabbit meat, pork, and bacon and cook on low heat in a pot of water, along with the two bouillon cubes. You can optionally add in some soup vegetables, like carrots, parsley, and onion, and dried mushrooms. After about 90 minutes, when the meat is soft, take it out and clean off any bones from the meat.

2. Use 1 cup of the leftover stock liquid and sauté the liver, cleaned and sliced into strips, for about 10 minutes.

3. Soak the bread rolls in another cup of the leftover stock.

4. Combine the meats and bread and mix in a food processor. Mix in eggs, herbs, spices, salt, and pepper.

5. Grease a loaf pan and place the meat pâté inside. The pâté should fill about three-quarters of the pan.

6. Bake in the oven at 400°F (200°C) for about 1 hour.

Deviled eggs

8 hardboiled eggs
4 mushrooms
1 cup (100 g) breadcrumbs
½ cup (125 ml) milk
2 tbsp diced dill
2 tbsp diced parsley
1 raw egg
salt and pepper

1. Peel and fry the mushrooms in some butter.

2. After cooking the eggs, cut them in half with a sharp knife and take out the egg yolks and egg whites.

3. Set aside 1 tablespoon of breadcrumbs and soak the rest in milk.

4. Dice the eggs and mix with diced mushrooms, dill, parsley, breadcrumbs and milk, salt, pepper, and one beaten egg.

5. Fill the halved egg shells, sprinkle some breadcrumbs on top, and fry in a skillet with butter on low heat with the tops touching the bottom of the skillet.

Serve hot or cold with sour cream or tartar sauce:

1. Take out the egg yolks from the hardboiled eggs and grate them on the fine slots of a grater.

2. Finely dice the mushrooms, pickles, and garlic cloves and mix all of the remaining ingredients until well-combined.

This sauce can be served with eggs, salads, meats, or sandwiches.

TARTAR SAUCE

4 hardboiled eggs
6 pickled mushrooms
2 pickles
2 garlic cloves
1 tbsp mustard
1 tbsp mayonnaise
2 tbsp sour cream
2 tsp lemon juice
salt and pepper

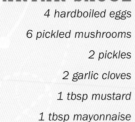

Vegetable salad

3 potatoes

3 carrots

2 apples

3 pickles

½ cup peas

½ cup (40 g) chopped walnuts

1 cup (250 ml) mayonnaise

1. Cook the potatoes and carrots so they are not too soft.

2. Dice the cooled potatoes and carrots, and apples and pickles into quarter-inch (6 mm) squares, and mix them gently in a salad bowl.

3. Add in the peas and walnuts.

4. Mix in mayonnaise and stir until evenly distributed.

To decorate, pour a quarter cup of mayonnaise on the top of the salad and garnish with peas, tomato wedges, radish slices, or walnuts. This salad looks great served on a lettuce-lined platter.

White borscht (biały barszcz)

13 oz (368 g) white kielbasa

½ cup (125 m) lemon juice, or pickle juice

dried herbs: bay leaf, marjoram

1 tbsp flour

½ cup (125 ml) sour cream

6 oz (170 g) kielbasa

salt and pepper

2 hardboiled eggs

1. Cook the white kielbasa in 2 quarts (2 l) of water for about 20 minutes. When the water starts to boil, take the kielbasa out.

2. On low heat, add lemon juice, dried herbs, salt and pepper.

3. Mix the flour with sour cream and 2 tablespoons of the broth, then mix in with the soup.

4. Take the soup off the heat and add in slices of kielbasa and wedges of hardboiled eggs.

Babka

1 packet active dry yeast
(¼ oz/7 g)
½ cup (115 g) sugar
1 cup (250 ml) milk
4 egg yolks
½ cup (115 g) butter
4 eggs
½ tsp salt
grated lemon peel
raisins, coated with flour
2½ cups (280 g) white flour

1. Mix yeast in lukewarm water and add half a teaspoon of sugar and a quarter cup of milk. Set aside in a warm place so the yeast will rise.

2. In a metal pot, beat together four egg yolks and a quarter of a cup of sugar on medium heat, until the mixture turns white and fluffy.

3. In a separate bowl, mix together 8 tablespoons of soft butter and the remaining ¼ cup of sugar. Gradually, add in the four eggs, one at a time, the beaten egg yolks, salt, raisins, grated lemon peel, yeast, and finally flour. The batter should be mixed for about half an hour, or until it glistens.

4. Set the batter aside in a warm area for half an hour until it rises. Then, pour it into a babka mold, or any cake mold, and place in a heated oven for an hour at 350°F (180°C).

Babka is usually decorated with sifted powdered sugar or icing. To make icing, mix 1 cup of powdered sugar with half a cup of lemon juice. Pour the icing on top of the cake and wait a couple of minutes until it hardens.

Cognac chocolate babka

1 cup (225 g) butter
2 cups (450 g) sugar
4 tbsp cocoa powder
½ cup (125 ml) water
4 eggs (whites and yolks separated)
2 cups (220) flour
1 tsp baking powder
almond extract
1 cup (80 g) raisins
3 tbsp cognac, or rum

1. Preheat the oven to 350°F (180°C).

2. In a saucepan on medium heat, melt the butter and mix with sugar, cocoa powder, and water until it boils. Set aside ½ cup to use as a glaze.

3. Beat the egg whites until stiff peaks form.

4. When the chocolate mass has cooled, stir in 4 egg yolks, flour mixed with baking powder, almond extract, raisins, cognac, and finally the beaten egg whites.

5. Bake in the oven for 45 minutes to 1 hour, and pour the glaze on top when the cake has cooled.

Marble babka

½ cup (115 g) butter
1 cup (225 g) sugar
2 eggs
2 cups (220 g) flour
1 tsp baking powder
¾ cup (190 ml) milk
lemon juice
¼ cup (30 g) cocoa powder

1. Preheat the oven to 325°F (160°C).

2. Beat the softened butter and sugar with an electric mixer until the batter is smooth and shiny.

3. In a separate bowl, beat the eggs, and in another bowl, mix the flour and baking powder.

4. Turn down the electric mixer to the lowest setting and gradually add in the beaten eggs.

5. Gradually add in the flour, milk, and 1 or 2 teaspoons of lemon juice.

6. When the batter is smooth and well-combined, divide it in two. Add the cocoa powder or melted bitter chocolate into one batter and mix well.

7. Grease a babka or loaf pan and alternate adding scoops from each batter.

8. Bake in the oven for 50 minutes.

Christmas Eve Baked carp

1 whole carp
1 tbsp butter
1 lemon
dried herbs
olive oil, or cooking oil
salt and pepper

1. Preheat the oven to 350°F (180°C).

2. Gut the fish, cut off the head, fins, and gills, and clean it, leaving the skin.

3. Grease the outside and inside of the fish with some butter. Cut a lemon into wedges and squeeze some of the juice over the fish, some on the inside, and leave the wedges inside the fish.

4. Sprinkle the inside of the fish with some dried herbs like thyme, oregano, basil, etc. Then sprinkle salt and pepper on the inside and outside.

5. Grease a glass baking dish with a couple of tablespoons of olive oil or cooking oil and place the fish in the dish, covering it with aluminum foil.

6. Bake in the middle of the oven for about 40 minutes, making sure the fish doesn't dry out.

If you'd like the fish to have a more striking presentation, only clean and gut the fish, leaving the head, fins, gill, and tail. You can decorate it with some lemon wedges, parsley, dill, mushrooms, or onions.

Rolled herring (rolmopsy)

1 jar of herring in vinegar

1 large onion

2 red or yellow bell peppers

1. Drain out the vinegar from the jar and lay out each individual herring piece.

2. Slice the onion horizontally. Then slice each onion ring in half. Place a couple of the onion slices on each piece of herring lengthwise.

3. Slice the peppers horizontally, slice each ring in half, and place lengthwise with the onion.

4. Roll each herring piece and fasten with a toothpick. You can serve these right away or chill in the refrigerator for a few hours.

Beet soup with ravioli

SOUP

2.5 oz (70 g) dried mushrooms

2 lb (900 g) beets

2 onions

herbs

sugar

salt and pepper

MUSHROOM-FILLED RAVIOLI

½ onion

1 tbsp breadcrumbs

2 eggs

salt and pepper

1⅓ cups (150 g) flour

1. In advance, soak the dried mushrooms in cold water for about 2 hours, then cook them in the same water until they turn soft, and drain, keeping the liquid and the mushrooms.

2. Prepare the ravioli: Make the filling by lightly frying the chopped onion. Add the finely diced mushrooms and bread-crumbs to the onion and fry for 3–5 minutes. After the filling cools down, beat in one egg and add salt and pepper to taste. To make the dough: Combine the flour and second egg and knead, adding a bit of water if the dough is too tough. Roll out the dough into a thin sheet and cut it into 2 x 2 inch (5 x 5 cm) squares.

3. Place filling by teaspoonfuls in the center of the dough, then fold the dough diagonally to make a triangle, sealing the edges. Then join the three corners and pinch them. Set the ravioli aside and make the soup.

4. Peel the beets and grate or dice them. Put the beets along with the chopped onion, dried herbs, salt, and pepper, into a pot with cold water and cook on medium heat until it boils. Drain and only retain the liquid. Mix the beet water with the broth from the previously cooked mushrooms, add in some sugar, salt, and cook until it boils.

5. In a separate pot, cook the ravioli on medium heat until they float to the top, then take them out, place them in the beet soup, and serve.

Christmas Eve dishes in Poland do not include any meat, so the ravioli filling is made with just mushrooms. On other occasions, however, cooked ground beef is added to the filling.

Greek-style fish

1 lb (900 g) fish fillets, such as
cod, haddock, herring, etc.

3 carrots

1 celery root

1 leek

fresh parsley

½ onion

2 tbsp cooking oil

6 oz (170 g) tomato paste

1 tbsp lemon juice, or vinegar

paprika

bay leaf

salt and pepper

1. Thaw the fish fillets, salt and pepper them, and fry them on both sides in cooking oil. Set aside.

2. Peel the carrots and celery root and grate them on the medium grating slots.

3. Finely chop the leek, parsley, and onion. Mix all of the vegetables together.

4. In a skillet or pot, heat the cooking oil, put in the chopped and grated vegetables along with two tablespoons of water, and sauté, covered, on medium heat until soft. At the end, add the tomato paste, lemon juice, paprika, bay leaf, salt, and pepper,

and stir everything, sautéing for a few more minutes. Set aside the vegetables to cool.

5. Cover the bottom of a glass dish with half of the fish fillets, add a layer of the vegetables on top, add a second layer of fish fillets, and top with the rest of the vegetables.

You can serve this dish cool or warm. To serve warm, fry the fish and sauté the vegetables at the same time in separate skillets and serve immediately, or follow the recipe above, grease the glass baking dish before layering the fish and vegetables, and warm up in the oven.

Sauerkraut and mushroom pierogies

Pierogi dough (see recipe on page 90)

2 oz (55 g) dried mushrooms

1 onion

1 tbsp butter

2 lb (900 g) sauerkraut

1 hardboiled egg

salt and pepper

1. In advance, soak the dried mushrooms in cold water for about 2 hours, then cook them in the same water until they turn soft. Drain, retaining the broth, and finely dice the mushrooms.

2. Finely dice the onion and fry with butter in a skillet, adding in finely diced sauerkraut and mushroom broth, and simmering until soft.

3. Finely dice the egg and add in to the sauerkraut along with the diced mushrooms. Season with salt and pepper and simmer on low heat for a few minutes.

4. Fill the pierogi dough and boil in salted water until they float to the top.

Mushroom sauce

1.8 oz (50 g) dried mushrooms
½ onion
2 tbsp butter
2 tbsp flour
2 tbsp sour cream
salt and pepper

1. In advance, soak the dried mushrooms in cold water for about 2 hours, then cook them in the same water, along with the onion and salt, until they turn soft. Drain, retaining the broth. Cut the mushroom and onion into thin slices.

2. Make a roux by lightly frying the flour in butter until the flour has some color. Add in sour cream along with the mushroom broth, sliced mushrooms, and onion and mix well. Salt and pepper and fry until it starts bubbling.

Serve this sauce with meats, pierogies, with groats, or any dumplings or pasta.

Sweet grain pudding (kutia)

1 cup wheatberries, or barley

4 tbsp honey

½ cup (115 g) sugar

2 cups (450 g) poppy seeds

bakalie (see recipe on page 109)

1. Rinse the wheatberries and leave to soak overnight.

2. Cook in water until the grains turn soft and drain on a sieve.

3. Mix the poppy seeds with honey, sugar, bakalie, and the wheatberries.

Poppyseed cake (makowiec)

1 packet active dry yeast
(¼ oz/7 g)

2 tbsp sugar

¼ cup (60 ml) milk

1 cup (110 g) flour

4 tbsp margarine, or butter

3 egg yolks

1 tsp salt

1 can of poppyseed filling
(14 oz/400 g)

½ cup (40 g) raisins

1 cup (110 g) powdered sugar

½ cup (125 ml) lemon juice

candied orange peel

1. Preheat the oven to 375°F (190°C).

2. Dissolve yeast with sugar in lukewarm milk and set aside to rise.

3. Mix the flour, melted margarine, egg yolks, salt, and the risen yeast and knead to make a dough. Roll it out into a half-inch (1.3 cm) thick rectangle.

4. Mix the poppy seed filling with raisins and spread it on the dough, leaving an inch-wide border along the edges. Roll the dough lengthwise and close up the sides of the log.

5. Grease a sheet of parchment paper and roll it around the log, leaving the sides open.

6. Bake for about 40 minutes.

7. To make icing, mix the powdered sugar with lemon juice to make a glaze and sprinkle candied orange on top.

Gingerbread cookies

3 tbsp honey

3 cups (330 g) flour

¾ cup (170 g) sugar

1 tsp baking soda

1 tbsp gingerbread spices
(or ground cinnamon, nutmeg,
ginger, and pepper)

1 egg

1. Preheat the oven to 325°F (160°C).

2. Melt the honey on low heat and mix it into the flour with a wooden spoon. Gradually add in sugar, baking soda, gingerbread spices, and one egg.

3. Knead the dough until smooth and roll out into a thin sheet with a rolling pin. Cut out shapes with a cookie cutter and place the cookies on a baking pan greased with butter or lined with parchment paper.

4. Bake in the oven for 10–15 minutes, until the cookies are golden brown.

You can sprinkle the cookies with powdered sugar or icing. To make icing, mix powdered sugar with lemon juice until you achieve a thick consistency. Spread the icing on the cooled cookies and wait a couple of minutes until the icing hardens.

Fruit cake (keks)

8 egg whites
2 cups (220 g) powdered sugar
2 cups (220 g) flour
½ cup (115 g) butter
1 tsp baking powder
½ cup (40 g) bakalie

1. Preheat the oven to 325°F (160°C).

2. Beat the egg whites. When they start to become fluffy, gradually add in the powdered sugar, and beat until stiff peaks form.

3. Gradually stir in flour, melted butter, and baking powder to the beaten egg whites. Mix the bakalie (see recipe on p. 109) with 1 tablespoon of flour and stir into the dough.

4. Pour the batter into a greased and floured loaf pan.

5. Bake in the oven for 40 minutes.

Compote with dried fruit

1 lb (450 g) dried fruit
(apples, pears, apricots,
bananas, etc.)

½ lb (225 g) dried prunes

1 tbsp sugar

⅓ cup (25 g) raisins

1 tbsp cloves

1 tsp cinnamon

optional: gelatin

1. Rinse the dried fruit with hot water, then leave to soak in 2 quarts (2 l) of cold water overnight.

2. The next day, take out the dried fruit and boil the remaining water adding sugar, raisins, cloves, and cinnamon and cook for 10 minutes. If you want, you can dissolve two packets of gelatin in hot water and add to the compote for a thicker consistency.

3. Pour over the dried fruit.

Instead of soaking the dried fruit overnight, you can also soak it for a few hours and then boil along with the rest of the ingredients for 10 minutes.

New Year's Eve Bacon-wrapped plums

10 dried plums, or dried prunes

caraway seeds

10 bacon strips

cooking oil

1. Soak the dried plums in cold water for a few hours until soft, then take out the pits.

2. Sprinkle some caraway seeds inside each plum.

3. Wrap each bacon strip around one plum and pierce with a toothpick.

4. Heat cooking oil in a skillet and fry the bacon-wrapped plums on high heat until golden brown on all sides.

Rolled ham

2 apples

3 tbsp sour cream, or plain yogurt

1 tbsp horseradish

3 tbsp raisins

salt and pepper

optional: chopped walnuts

15 ham slices

1. Clean, peel, and grate the apples on the bigger grating slots of a grater.

2. Mix the sour cream and horseradish, and stir with the apples and raisins, adding salt and pepper to taste. You can add some chopped walnuts for a crunchy texture.

3. Place the filling on each slice of ham, roll it, and fasten with a toothpick and tie with a cooked leaf of a leek.

Serve on a platter lined with lettuce leaves.

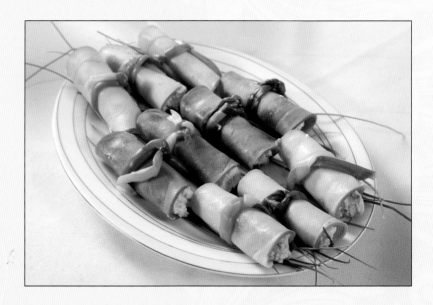

Chicken salad

4 chicken breasts

3 tbsp mayonnaise

3 tbsp sour cream, or plain yogurt

1 can pineapple chunks

2 tbsp chopped walnuts

⅓ cup (25 g) raisins

parsley

salt

1. Fry the chicken breasts on a skillet with cooking oil until brown, and cut into bite-size pieces.

2. Mix together mayonnaise and sour cream.

3. In a bowl, mix the chicken pieces, pineapple chunks, walnuts, raisins, and cream. Sprinkle with chopped parsley and add salt to taste.

You can sprinkle the salad with some cheddar cheese and eat as a side or a on a sandwich.

Hunter's stew (bigos)

2 oz (56 g) dried mushrooms, or
fresh mushrooms

1 cabbage head

½ lb (225 g) beef

½ lb (225 g) pork

1-2 onions

¼ lb (115 g) bacon

½ lb (225 g) kielbasa

24 oz (680 g) sauerkraut, rinsed

dried herbs: oregano,
bay leaf, thyme

salt and pepper

optional: 2 apples, prunes,
1 cup broth, 1 cup wine

1. If using dried mushrooms or prunes, soak them overnight.

2. Dice the cabbage head, cut the beef and pork into small cubes, and boil in water until soft. If using fresh mushrooms, chop them and add at the end of cooking time. Drain the water.

3. Dice the onions and bacon and fry on a skillet until lightly browned.

4. In a large pot, mix the boiled cabbage, beef, pork, sliced kielbasa, rinsed sauerkraut, fried bacon and onions, chopped mushrooms and prunes, herbs, salt, and pepper and cook on medium heat for about 1 hour, stirring occasionally. You can optionally add diced or roughly grated apples, or some broth or wine for taste.

This dish can be made in a number of ways. You can make it without the cabbage, only using the sauerkraut, and you can use any combination of meats. You can also fry the beef, pork, and mushrooms, instead of cooking them in water.

Three-layer walnut-almond-chocolate cake

WALNUT LAYER

5 eggs (whites and yolks separated)

⅔ cup (150 g) sugar

⅔ cup (150 g) ground walnuts

1 tsp baking powder

ALMOND LAYER

5 eggs (whites and yolks separated)

⅔ cup (150 g) ground almonds

⅔ cup (150 g) sugar

1 tsp baking powder

CHOCOLATE LAYER

5 eggs (whites and yolks separated)

1 cup (110 g) flour

1 tbsp cocoa powder

⅔ cup (150 g) sugar

1 tsp baking powder

1. Prepare the first walnut layer: Beat the 5 egg whites, gradually adding in sugar, until white and fluffy. Then, beat in 1 egg yolk at a time. Mix in the ground walnuts, baking powder, and bake in a greased cake pan at 350°F (180°C) for about 25 minutes.

2. Prepare the second almond layer: Follow the same directions as for the first layer, but substitute the walnuts with almonds.

WALNUT FILLING

½ cup (100 g) finely ground walnuts

½ (60 g) cup powdered sugar

¼ cup (60 ml) sour cream

CHOCOLATE CREAM

⅓ cup (40 g) powdered sugar

½ cup (115 g) butter

1 tbsp water

1 tbsp cocoa powder

1 tsp vodka, or liquor

3. Prepare the third chocolate layer: Follow the same directions as for the first layer, but substitute the walnuts with flour and cocoa powder.

4. Prepare the walnut filling by mixing all of the ingredients. Prepare the chocolate cream according to the directions on page 161. Place the walnut filling between the cakes and spread the chocolate cream around the entire cake.

Index

COOKING NOTES